PYROGRAPHY
Workbook

BY SUE WALTERS

FOX CHAPEL
PUBLISHING

Acknowledgements:

Special thanks to Gayle and Barb for their help in proofreading.

Special thanks to Razertip Industries Inc. for providing the chart information on page 42.

ISBN 978-1-56523-258-7

Publisher's Cataloging-in-Publication Data

Walters, Sue.

   Pyrography workbook / by Sue Walters. -- East Petersburg, PA : Fox
Chapel Publishing, Inc., 2005.

     p. ; cm.
     ISBN: 978-1-56523-258-7

     1. Pyrography. 2. Etching. 3. Woodwork. I. Title.

TT199.8 .W35 2005

745.51/4--dc22   0505

To learn more about the other great books from Fox Chapel Publishing, or to find a retailer near you, call toll-free 800-457-9112 or visit us at *www.FoxChapelPublishing.com*.

Note to Authors: We are always looking for talented authors to write new books. Please send a brief letter describing your idea to Acquisition Editor, 1970 Broad Street, East Petersburg, PA 17520.

Printed in China
Twelfth printing

Dedication

This book is dedicated with love, thanks,
and deep appreciation to the following people:

My Mother, Alison Walters
Gayle Martin
Barb Kaminski

You make the impossible seem possible.
Thank you for your help, support, belief, and love.

And to The Boys, who look out for me.
I love you both.

TABLE OF CONTENTS

ABOUT THE AUTHOR

SUE WALTERS

is a self-taught, internationally renowned, and award-winning pyrographic artist. After a career in horticulture, Sue began her pyrographic journey after receiving a burner as a present. She soon started designing and burning souvenirs for the Australian tourist industry. Her focus then shifted to extensively experimenting with various types of pyrographic techniques, eventually specializing in the areas of high realism, wildlife, and miniature burning.

Sue's passion for pursuing all that pyrography has to offer continues to this day, and she remains dedicated to passing on her knowledge to other aspiring burners.

A fifth-generation Aussie, Sue was born in 1962 and still calls Australia home.

Introduction

Pyrography, meaning to draw with fire, was fashionable in the Victorian and the Art Deco periods and is now experiencing an exciting new wave of popularity and innovation. Whether this is due to the development of modern burning tools or simply because its time has come again is hard to tell. One thing is certain: Pyrography fascinates people.

In its most basic form, the appeal of pyrography lies in its rustic and natural beauty. In its most complex form, the combination of texture and drawing can create pictures that appear almost lifelike. Add the use of color and the wide varieties of wood and materials that can be used, and you begin to see that the possibilities for burning are almost endless, no matter what direction you choose to take.

For some people, the thought of a large horizon of possibilities is exciting; others find that prospect more than a little daunting, and rather than flying blind, they would prefer someone to help show them the way. That's where I come in. My aim is to help both the beginner and advanced burner make the most of pyrography, to demystify burning, and to make it a more enjoyable experience.

Whether you want to take up pyrography as a hobby, use it as part of your craft, or simply get more use of your burner than signing your name, it is my hope that this book not only teaches you sound practical advice but also inspires you and opens your eyes to new and exciting possibilities.

Together we'll explore special nib techniques and learn how to apply them in a series of step-by-step projects. We'll also look at textures and patterns, unusual pyrographical variations, and how to burn on leather and other materials. Color can accent and complement pyrographic work, so I've dedicated a chapter to this subject also.

This book wouldn't be complete without covering the practical and necessary aspects of safety and work area setup. Timber selection, preparation, and pattern transfer will be discussed along with a look at the various types of burning tools that are available in today's market. Finally, a selection of patterns is provided to help inspire future burning.

Pyrography is a wonderful craft. There are few art forms in this world that offer the unique combination of being able to see what you draw as well as feel it. There are few craft tools that are so versatile as to be able to move from decorating furniture, to texturing a carved duck, to making a decorative piece of wall art. Pyrography can do all that and more. It has given me endless hours of enjoyment, and I hope it will give you the same.

—Sue Walters

Gallery

Here's Looking at You, pyrography and acrylic paint on mallee. To enable pyrography to stand out on dark wood, color can be used to accent the burning. In this case, acrylic paint has been used on top of the pyrography to accent the owl's face. (See Chapter 12: Color, page 102.) 10 inches by 12 inches.

© Sue Walters

Koala, monochrome pyrography on basswood. To create the soft appearance of Koala fur, this piece was made up of thousands of burnt dots. (See the Fluffy Fur section, page 98.) 12 inches by 9 inches.

Platypus Diving, monochrome pyrography on silky oak. Bark-edged slabs of timber can give a natural frame and an interesting platform for some pyrography. This large piece was relief carved before burning to help create an illusion of realism. (See the Relief Carving section, page 34.) Note that the shape of the wood has been carefully considered when choosing the subject matter. 39 inches by 20 inches.

Charging Elephant, monochrome pyrography on cowhide. Leather burning requires a cooler heat than timber pyrography. The smell can be a little strong for some people, but the ease of burning more than makes up for this small shortcoming. (See the Leather section, page 26.) 11 inches by 8 inches.

S.A.WALTERS

Wedge Tail Eagle, pyrography and oil paint wash on cowhide. Many types of pigment can be combined with leather pyrography to great effect. In this case, a thin wash of artist oil paint, suspended in mineral spirits, was applied to the piece after it was burned. (See the Leather section, page 26.) 13 inches by 9 inches.

Eagle Owl, monochrome pyrography on rag paper. Burning on paper is much easier than most people think. Because paper is always available and provides a white platform, this kind of pyrography is a viable and effective alternative to timber burning. (See the Paper section, page 27.) 8 inches by 5 inches.

© Sue Walters

Gum Leaves, monochrome pyrography on basswood round. Burning a dark background around a design provides a strong contrast, allowing the picture to stand out. (See the Negative Pyrography section, page 33.) 12 inches by 9 inches.

© Sue Walters

Turtle Rising, monochrome pyrography on silky oak. Just as in *Platypus Diving,* this piece was relief carved before pyrography commenced. A heavy-duty skew was used to create all of the stop cuts before the excess timber was carved away with a chisel. (See the Relief Carving section, page 34.) 22 inches by 19 inches.

© Sue Walters

Grazing Deer, pyrography, watercolor wash, and gouache on rag paper. Color, combined with paper burning, can look very effective. In this case, watercolor paint was used on the background while acrylic paint was used on the deer. The grass was textured with a rotary tool and burr. 10 inches by 8 inches.

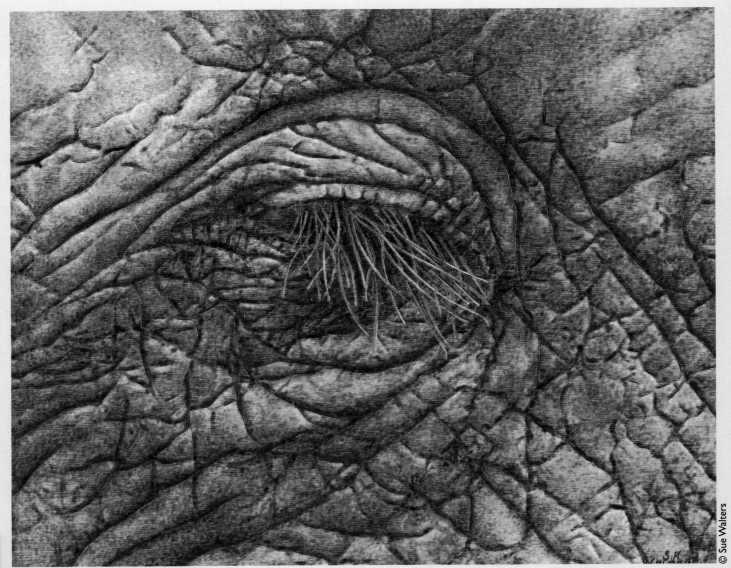

Elephant Eye, monochrome pyrography on birch plywood. As in *Koala* (on page 2), this piece was almost entirely created with thousands of burnt dots. Here, the many layers of dots helped to create a leathery and rough effect. (See the Leathery Skin section, page 99.) 11 inches by 8 inches.

© Sue Walters

Equipment, Work Area, and Safety

Woodburning Machines

A woodburner, of course, is a critical piece of equipment for pyrographic work. (See **Figure 1A**.) Like all woodworking tools, however, the choice of which woodburner to use is a personal one that depends on a variety of factors. In this chapter, you will learn about the various types of pyrographic machines, their features, and what might be suitable for you. We will also look at a typical work area setup, explore the additional equipment needed, and consider safe pyrographic practices.

Locating a Pyrographic Machine

Selecting a woodburner should be as simple as choosing the best tool that suits your particular needs. I wish it were that straightforward, but in fact, your location may actually limit your choice before you even start looking at the pros and cons of each individual machine.

I am often contacted by people who are eager to start burning but are finding it difficult to find a machine—any machine, let alone the one that might suit them best. The truth is that pyrography is a minority craft. Our equipment is sparse compared to other woodworking and craft products.

That doesn't mean it's not out there and that excellent tools aren't available, it just means that you need to know where to look and accept that certain limitations might govern your decision making.

Woodburning has developed quite differently in North America compared to British, Australian, and European areas. This means that the general design of handles and nibs can vary in each region.

Pyrography in North America has mainly grown up in the woodcarving fraternity as a means of texturing decoys and other wildlife carvings. This has led manufacturers to create burners with small handles and a vast array of nibs capable of burning a myriad of textures in confined spaces.

The roots of pyrography in Europe and Australia were, and still are, much more focused on flat artwork and on the decoration of furniture and turnings. It is seen more as an aesthetic pastime, a way of burning pictures with fire rather than texturing wood. Designed to keep the hand cool while burning for long periods of time on hard surfaces, handles in these areas tend to be larger than their North American counterparts. The nibs have not developed past their intended drawing

© Sue Walters

Figure 1A: A typical variable-temperature pyrographic machine comes with an on/off switch and a dial to adjust nib temperature. "Dual Units," as illustrated above, have the option of using two pens on the one machine. A toggle switch controls which pen is in use.

purpose, so they lack the variety of those found in North America.

But all is not lost. If you really want a burner from another country that has all the features you want, it may be made available to you. Some manufacturers are now catering to international customers by providing units that can be used in other countries. Of course, imported tools will invariably cost you more than those locally made. If you want an imported burner, contact the manufacturer or distributor directly and organize shipment by mail or you might be able to find a local company that stocks that brand. In any event, the manufacturer will be able to advise you of availability. (See the Resources section on page 138 for a list of manufacturers.)

If you don't have access to the Internet or if you don't wish to go to too much trouble, the most likely place to find woodburning equipment is at specialist woodworking or woodcarving supply shops. Most will usually stock a limited selection of one or two brands of variable-temperature

burners and associated products, and some will even let you try before you buy. Some of these stores will also stock the basic set-temperature burners.

Other places you can find pyrography tools and products include craft supply outlets and major retail chains. The units sold there usually fall under the solid point category. They look like soldering irons, are cheaper than variable-temperature burners, are usually set to one temperature, and are generally directed toward the hobbyist. Some of these irons are of a quality and temperature that allow very decent pyrography to be done. There are, however, some extremely cheap irons that flood the market now and then. They are usually poor quality, and the nib temperature is so low that effective burning is either almost impossible or painfully slow.

More than anything, the Internet has opened up the world of pyrography. Not only has it allowed people to see other pyrographic art, but it has also opened their eyes to the features available on other pyrographic machines. With this has come a demand for manufacturers to begin offering these features as options to their standard machines. For instance, many British and Australian-style machines only have a few writing nibs available. People in these areas are now asking that the manufacturer provide a larger range of nib designs because, after viewing North American systems, they would like this option rather than having to make their own nibs or purchase different burners.

Conversely, some North American manufacturers are now supplying pens that take plain nichrome (nickel/chromium) wire so that their customers can fashion their own nibs at a fraction of the cost they normally pay.

General Considerations

Generally speaking, pyrography machines fall into two categories: solid point, set-temperature machines and wire nib, variable-temperature machines. Even though both types are designed to do the same thing, they are very different. Before you buy a burner, I advise you to consider the following three points:

1) Cost: How much do you want to spend?

2) Time: What and how much you intend to burn?

3) Features: What features would you like the burner to have?

Solid Point Burners

At around a third or less of the cost of a wire burner, solid point burners are far less expensive to buy. Solid point burners look much like a soldering iron but are specially designed for woodburning. (See **Figure 1B**.) There is a temptation for some people to buy a soldering iron, but be prepared for disappointment if you go this route, as they rarely burn hot enough to be effective nor do they have the correct nib shapes. The nibs of solid point burners are larger than those of wire burners and are often shaped from rods of copper or brass. They either slide or screw into the heating element. The handles tend to be larger than those of wire burners, and your hand is held further back from your work.

A decent quality solid point burner will burn most woods except those that are very hard. Because most are set on one temperature only, you need to adjust your hand speed to alter the darkness of your work. The faster you move the burner, the lighter the mark, and the slower you move the burner, the darker the mark.

Generally speaking, solid point burners aren't as capable of doing the detailed work of a wire nib. They are especially good for broad, large-scale work, but I've also seen some excellent examples of small to medium-scale work.

There are a couple of solid point burners available that feature variable heat adjustment, but they also take minutes to warm up and are much more expensive than irons with set temperatures.

Wire Nib Burners

Wire nib burners generally fall into two categories: the factory-made nib style of North America and the hot-wire style of Britain/Europe and Australia. Both types have a power box that has an on/off switch and a dial that allows you to change the temperature of the nib. Nibs are heated when electricity is passed through a wire and can usually be red-hot

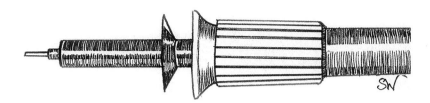

Figure 1B: A solid point, set-temperature pyrographic burner looks somewhat like a soldering iron. A solid nib is heated by an element, and the temperature can't be adjusted.

Figure 1C: The nichrome wire nibs of the European-style pyrographic pen are usually held in place by two screws.

within seconds. Cool down time is nearly as fast. A handle or pyrographic pen is connected to the power box via a cord, and the nib is located at the end. This is where the two types start to differ.

European-Style Burners

European-style handles tend to be connected to the power source by a solder joint, and the nibs are held in place on the handle by two screws. (See **Figure 1C**.) Nibs can be changed by loosening the connection screws, swapping the nib, then re-tightening. The screws provide a snug contact for smooth conduction.

The range of nibs made by each manufacturer can be limited; however, the nib wire for these units is cheap to buy and can be made into various shapes by the owner. This can be a deterrent for people who require specialized nibs to achieve life-like textures on their wildlife carvings, but for most flat and decorative burners, a basic set of skew, shader, and writing nibs is all that is needed to achieve what they want. Even the humble nib of bent hot wire can produce remarkable results!

North-American-Style Burners

North American pyrography pens come in two styles: interchangeable nib and fixed nib. Regardless of the pen style, connection to the power base is also by cord, but generally the cords

Figure 1D: The North-American-style pyrographic pens tend to come with a large variety of factory made nibs. The nibs are either slotted or soldered in place.

aren't soldered in place; instead they are attached by either jacks or screws.

Most North American interchangeable nibs are simply slotted into place on two posts at the end of the handle. Because it's not necessary to buy a new handle when you want a new nib, they are far less expensive than fixed nibs, but the poor performance of most interchangeable nibs negates the financial benefit. Because there is less efficient conduction with the connection of the inter-changeable nibs, the heat can fluctuate and the handle can get quite hot. A slotted interchange-able-nib system might be better suited to someone who is intending to burn only in very short spells or to sign their name. For the keen pyrographer, solder or screw connections produce far better, more consistent results.

Some North American companies now manu-facture a pen that has screw contacts to allow people to interchange homemade and factory nibs. Changing over screw nibs might take a little longer than the slotted variety but the improved conduction may well make it worth the effort.

The burning tip of a fixed-nib pen is soldered in place, providing a better electrical connection than the previous types. (See **Figure 1D**.) Fixed nibs are, by far, more reliable than interchange-able nibs, but they are also more expensive. Each time you want a new style of nib you will have to buy a whole new pen.

Features to Consider

Once you've decided on the type of pyrographic tool you want, you might want to consider some features before you make your final purchase.

Solid point, set-temperature burners are pretty straightforward with only a few variations. Some companies offer burners in a range of wattage,

and obviously, the higher the wattage, the hotter it burns. (Anything below 20 watts can be quite slow.) Also, make sure the burners come with a decent variety of nib shapes and that you can buy replacements or perhaps different designs if you need to.

Wire nib, variable-temperature machines offer a lot more variety. It can be a little daunting to know what to ask about or consider when com-paring features, so I've prepared a small guideline to help you find your way.

Power: Have enough power for your needs. If you plan to do a lot of burning on extremely hard wood, you will need a machine with plenty of grunt. There should be no fluctuation in burning temperature once the nib is on the surface. It is natural for the nib to be slightly hotter on first contact with the surface, but the burn should be consistent once the nib is down and traveling. When the nib is again lifted, the heat should recover to the nib almost immediately.

Handle: The handle must be as comfortable and as cool as possible. A hot handle simply dis-tracts you from what should be an enjoyable experience. As a personal preference, I find foam grips make long burning sessions more comfort-able. Some companies supply extra foam grips or vented covers for their handles.

Dual handle: Some machines are capable of having two handles plugged in at once. Usually, only one pen at a time can be used (toggled by a switch), but it's a handy feature to have and saves you the time and the wear and tear of swapping out pens when you want to change a nib.

Warranty and service: Naturally, make sure there is adequate warranty and service covering your burner. Ask about machine repair should there be a problem. A lot of companies will have a pen repair service at minimal cost and can also make a nib from your own design.

Heavy-duty and standard pens: Some compa-nies offer heavy-duty pens as well as standard pens. Standard pens are for delicate to normal burning; heavy-duty pens can take extra punishment and require 16-gauge cord, which is usually supplied.

Temperature dial: Some units come with low-end temperature adjustment. This allows you to turn the heat down farther if the first setting is still too hot. This feature is a nice addition if you are using your burner to sculpt wax, but is not necessary for general woodburning.

On/off indicator: A light indicator is essential to avoid leaving your burner on by mistake.

Adaptors: Pen and jack adaptors that allow you to use other brands of pens are available for some North American machines. This can be a handy feature if you want to change power bases without wasting your old pens or if you want to buy a style of nib not available in your own brand.

Solid Point and Wire Nib Burners Pros and Cons

Solid Point Burner Pros

- Inexpensive to buy
- More readily available
- Nibs are not easily damaged
- Nibs can be easily made
- Good for medium to large-scale work
- Branding stamps can be an optional extra for some burners

Solid Point Burner Cons

- Nibs are slow to heat up and cool down (up to 5 minutes)
- Large handle
- Heating element below the handle is extremely hot
- Usually no on/off switch
- Burns wood at a slower rate; is more time consuming to burn with
- Hand is farther away from work
- Less control for delicate work
- Not capable of extremely detailed work
- Can burn out after a lot of use

Wire Nib Pros

- Capable of very delicate work
- Capable of burning the hardest of woods
- Nibs cool rapidly and take a matter of seconds to heat
- Most units can dial a range from cool to red-hot
- Includes on/off switch
- Burns wood more quickly; is less time consuming to burn with
- Easy nib changes
- Owners of European-style machines can make their own inexpensive nibs from Nichrome wire
- Owners of North-American-style machines can choose from a huge range of factory-made nibs

Wire Nib Cons

- More expensive to buy
- Not readily found; sometimes mail order is necessary
- Repair can be more difficult or expensive if purchase point is not local
- Fixed-nib pens of North American models can be expensive
- Interchangeable-nib pens can be unreliable
- Nib size and strength is limited by the gauge of wire
- Nibs are more easily damaged

Figure 1E: A pyrographic machine, nib cleaning materials, practice board and a blade are all that are needed for the basic pyrographic setup.

Other Equipment and Setup

The setup of your work area basically consists of a pyrographic machine, a nib cleaner, a practice board, and a blade. (See **Figure 1E**.) The following is a list of the other equipment you will need in your kit for various stages of pyrography projects. (We'll have a look at any other special equipment you might need in its relevant section.)

- **Light source:** Usually shines from the direction opposite your drawing hand.
- **Sandpaper:** To prepare the surface of the timber.
- **Rag or tack cloth:** To clean away dust.
- **Scrap material:** For practicing your strokes and testing the temperature of the nib. (Use the same material as the main project.)
- **Tin lid of an old jar:** For holding warm nibs.
- **Old sheet of plywood:** To place on a workbench as protection from scorches.
- **Nib-cleaning materials:** See Chapter 5 for suggestions.
- **Pliers:** For removing hot nibs from solid point and interchangeable wire burners.

- **Leaning board to tilt work:** As simple as a piece of plywood leaning against some books.
- **Sharp blade:** For picking out highlights, erasing mistakes, cutting patterns, sharpening blades, and cleaning stubborn carbon from nibs.
- **Graphite paper:** To transfer a design or pattern.
- **Tracing paper:** Another method to transfer designs.
- **Tape:** For holding patterns down during transfer.
- **Fine red ballpoint pen:** For transferring patterns. (Red is more easily seen over black pattern lines.)
- **Scissors:** For cutting paper.
- **Ruler:** For ruling straight lines and measuring.
- **#2B pencil:** Soft enough to erase, for drawing on wood without leaving an impression.
- **Pencil sharpener:** To sharpen pencils.
- **Eraser:** Gum or other soft eraser.
- **Varnish:** Spray or brush on, to protect your work after completion. (See Chapter 3 for suggestions.)

Figure 1F: Breeze can disrupt the consistency of nib heat. It's better to position a fan to pull smoke away from your project, rather than across it.

Safety

To prevent harm coming to the pyrographer, a few rules of safety should be observed.

• Never use treated or sealed wood for pyrography. Burning treated wood can produce toxic fumes.

• Never use medium-density fiberboard (MDF), man-made boards, or other bonded material for pyrography. They can be made of toxic materials, and the fumes, if inhaled, can cause serious health problems.

• Natural cork can be used, but be careful of cork sheeting, as sometimes it can be impregnated with a resinous binder to improve the durability. If you burn plywood be careful not to burn deep into the glue layer.

• Many pyrographic techniques produce little or no smoke, but there is no denying that sometimes a little wood smoke is produced,

especially when you have your nib heat set on high. Obviously, a dust collection or ventilation system is best to extract smoke, but the average hobbyist usually will not have access to one. There are several other alternatives to prevent breathing smoke.

1) Use a fan, pointed away from your work, to suck the smoke away. The air from a fan pointed at your work can affect the nib temperature, resulting in inconsistent burning. (See **Figure 1F**.) The same can happen with a draft from a window.

2) Work in a well ventilated room.

3) Make sure your head stays far back from your work. Tilting your work by placing it on a sloped surface will allow you to keep your head back and still see your work.

4) You can use your breath to gently blow away a stream of smoke as long as you don't blow directly on the nib.

5) Masks and smoke filtration systems are another option; however, it must be kept in mind that smoke particles are extremely minute and aver-

age filters will not trap them. A dust mask will certainly not be sufficient, and only those masks and filtration systems rated to capture smoke will be adequate. Please ask a specialist for further advice.

- Always turn your burner off when you're not working. It's easy to get distracted and forget it's still on.

- Place your project on a slope to keep your hand angled away from heat rising from the nib.

- Even though hot-cutting polystyrene is a recommended side use for some burning units, I do not recommend it. This material contains some chemicals that I believe could be hazardous to one's immediate and long-term health. I am equally wary of acrylic resin (the plastic-type sheeting that looks like glass). Some pyrographers advocate burning this material, but I would strongly urge caution. The same goes for using sanding sealers on wood and then burning.

  There are other materials you might be tempted to burn at times. Before you do, question your choice. If it isn't a natural product, think twice. When in doubt, ask the manufacturer for a Material Safety Data Sheet (MSDS). These sheets aren't always readily available, but a search on the Internet will invariably find the MSDS information you are looking for.

- If you have a solid point, set-temperature burner, be aware that the heating element can get extremely hot and that you should keep your hand well away from this area.

- Never burn near water.

- Always turn off the iron to change nibs.

- Always wear a dust mask when sanding.

- Don't leave children unattended around a burner—they are fascinated by pyrography.

- There are some techniques that encourage the pyrographer to burn on top of pigments. It is still unknown if there is general danger in this practice, so take care in choosing the types of pigments to burn over. Avoid paints and pigments that contain lead and other metals such as cadmium, as well as any that contain arsenic and other chemicals. Do not burn on a surface painted with acrylic paints. Ask the manufacturer or your art supplier if you are unsure.

- Leather and animal hides are wonderful to work on, but please use only vegetable-tanned leather. Chromium-tanned leather can produce dangerous fumes. (Chromium leather often appears more soft and supple.)

- If the cord or handle of your burner gets hot and you are getting little or no heat to the nib, turn off the unit and check all of the connections to see if they are firmly plugged or screwed in. If the problem persists (and especially if there is a buzzing noise), I suggest you contact the manufacturer for advice before further use.

- When resting your burning pen, use the holder provided to prevent an accident.

- Lastly, some heavy sapwoods, such as cedar, can cause irritation to a small percentage of people. If you burn on a wood that seems to upset you, please discontinue using it.

Preparation and Transfer

Good preparation is essential to producing consistent pyrographic results. In this chapter, you will learn how to prepare a timber surface and the various ways to transfer a design to your project.

Preparing the Wood

Pyrography is a physical craft. To burn a line of even color, the nib must travel across the surface at an even, consistent speed. To help us achieve this, the timber for pyrography work needs to be fine sanded so that the nib can travel smoothly across the surface with as little resistance as possible.

Hand sanding is the cheapest method but not always the easiest. For larger projects or when I need to do several pieces, I use either an inverted belt sander or a random orbital (eccentric) sander. Yes, these machines can cost a little bit to buy initially but, believe me, if the wood needs a fair bit of work, they can sure cut down on effort and save enormous chunks of time.

A linisher is like a slow-moving, bench-mounted belt sander, and it's ideal for straight-edged projects, like signs. It's also perfect for sanding small objects like refrigerator magnets and key ring blanks—objects where it is easier to place the blank on the sander, rather than the sander on the blank. (This also applies to hand sanding small objects.)

A random orbital sander is easy to use and won't run away from the work or damage the wood like a disc sander can. Flat orbital, mouse, and palm sanders will also do a decent job. I find a little touch of hand sanding with 400/600-grit (extra fine) sandpaper is sometimes necessary if you want a super-fine finish or need to eliminate any swirl marks after machine sanding.

For small projects, I hand sand with either a sanding block or a sanding pad. Sanding blocks are more suitable for flat surfaces and can be as simple as a block of wood with sandpaper wrapped around it, or, to make life easier, you can buy foam blocks at your hardware store that are impregnated with abrasive material. Sanding pads are more flexible and are excellent for sanding round objects or spot sanding small areas.

Once you have finished sanding, wipe down the surface with an old rag or tack cloth, and you're ready to transfer your design.

Placing the Design

When placing the design, orientate it to suit the shape and grain of the wood. If the direction of your design is landscape, or horizontal, it's better to lay the pattern on the wood so that the grain runs horizontally across the picture. You can then incorporate the grain or features of the wood into the picture. For instance, some grain can help to accentuate items like cloud patterns, water, the ground, or stripes on a zebra.

Faults in the wood can also be utilized to help the piece, rather than hinder it. A knot in the wood can become a depression in a tree or a fallen log. Spalting, a fungal discoloration of the timber, can become an evening sky or an angry sea.

Because wood can burn differently depending on its density, it's also a good point to remember to avoid placing the main subject of your drawing halfway across two different parts of timber. For example, if you are burning a picture of a horse and you have half of it over a hard patch of grain and half over a soft patch, you will end up with two distinctly different-looking halves of a horse.

Transferring the Design

Careful transfer of a design will give the pyrogra-pher a clear "map" to follow when the burning begins. The following methods outline some of the ways this can be accomplished.

Tracing: I recommend never using carbon paper to transfer your pattern or design. Lines traced with carbon can bleed on contact with heat and are difficult, if not impossible, to erase. If you do choose to use carbon paper, sand the transferred pattern enough so that a faint line is all that is left. (See **Figure 2A** and **Figure 2B**.) Black graphite paper won't bleed and can be erased or sanded to lighten an area that has transferred too darkly. A 2B pencil can darken any lines that are too faint. Graphite paper also comes in white, which is handy if you want to trace a design on very dark or pre-burnt wood.

Heat transfer: If a pattern is made with a laser printer or photocopier, it can be placed face down, and when heat is applied to the back, the pattern will be transferred to the surface underneath. (See **Figure 2C** and **Figure 2D**.) The drawback of this method is that the image will be the reverse of the original. If you want the image to be an exact copy of the original, you will have to flip the image on your computer or on a photocopy machine before transfer.

A shading nib turned up quite high and rubbed

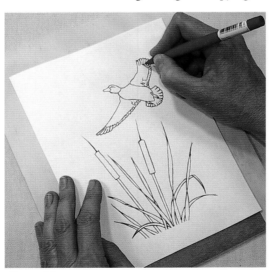

Figure 2A
Tracing
1) Place the pattern face up.
2) Tape the pattern in position.
3) Place graphite paper between the pattern and the object.
4) Test that the graphite paper is right side down.
5) Trace the pattern with a 2H pencil or a red fine ballpoint pen.
6) Lightly sand the design if the transferred image is too dark. If it is too light, darken it with a 2B pencil.

Figure 2B

Figure 2C
Heat Transfer
1) Place the pattern face down on the object.
2) Tape the pattern in position.
3) Use a shading nib or a clothes iron to heat the back of the pattern.
4) Sand lightly if the image appears too dark. (Faint lines are preferable to dark lines because they won't show in the finished project.)

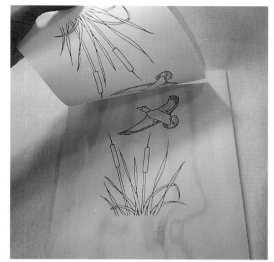

Figure 2D

along the lines of the pattern gives an extremely crisp transfer. A clothes iron (without the steam on) can also be used, but I've found that the toe of the iron, not just the base, needs to be rubbed firmly over the pattern to prevent a patchy transfer. Freshly printed paper works best. Lightly sand off excess darkness after the transfer, leaving just a faint pattern.

Spirit transfer: Laser printed or photocopied images can be transferred by placing the images face down and rubbing mineral spirits on the back. The spirits dissolve the ink, which is then transferred to the surface underneath. (See **Figure 2E** and **Figure 2F**.) If you want the image to be

Figure 2E
Spirit Transfer
1) Place the pattern face down on the object.
2) Tape the pattern in place.
3) Use a brush or your fingers to moisten paper with mineral spirits.
4) Push down to transfer the ink image.
5) Peel the paper away and allow the wood to dry thoroughly.
6) Lightly sand if the image has transferred too darkly.

Figure 2F

an exact copy of the original, you will have to flip the image on your computer or on a photocopy machine before transferring.

The spirit transfer method is faster than the heat transfer method, but a little messier. I also found that the image wasn't as crisp and that there was a tendency for an image to bleed if you are a little heavy-handed with the rubbing. Let the spirit evaporate and lightly sand the pattern so that only a light image remains before you burn.

Patterns

It is not necessary to be an artist to do pyrography. In fact, like other crafts, most people who burn do so from the patterns and designs of others. It can be difficult to obtain or buy patterns for pyrography if you don't know where to look, but here are a few suggestions: folk art pattern books, sketch books, lead lighting patterns, pattern CDs, carving patterns, and clip art. There are

also an increasing number of patterns specifically dedicated to pyrography where both a line pattern and tonal picture are provided.

Many types of black and white art could also give you inspiration. Some suggestions are pencil art, black-and-white photography, charcoal art, geometric patterns, Celtic art, cartoons, pen-and-ink art, lithographs, etchings, and other forms of print medium.

Lastly, a search on the Internet for either "pyrographic patterns" or "woodburning patterns" will harvest many choices. For simple burning projects, the Internet also has many clip art sites that have images to download.

Making Your Own Patterns

You can easily make your own patterns from photographs as long as they are copyright-free or taken by you. The copyright law automatically protects most images and artwork. This means you can't use the image for your own profit without permission of the owner. There are many places however, especially on the Internet, where you can find copyright-free images to download. You can also purchase images, patterns books, and CDs.

Once you find a photo or an image from which you would like to make a pattern, you can download it or scan it into your computer and then resize it to the size you want. It can then be printed and used immediately as a pattern. (I recommend using graphite paper to transfer it.) You could also use tracing paper to copy the basic elements of the picture or use a photocopier. To prevent ruining pictures from a pattern book, you could scan them and use the printouts for transferring the picture instead of the original.

Remember, when you are making your own patterns from a photograph, it's not necessary to trace every little detail of the picture. (See **Figure 2G**.) In the pattern to the left, you'll see that I've only drawn the main features of the wolf as well as mapped in the direction of the fur with little pen strokes. You'll also notice that I haven't used solid pen lines to draw the edges of the wolf. When tracing the outline of an animal, it's better to indicate the edge by flicking strokes in the direction of the fur, rather than drawing a solid line.

© Sue Walters

Figure 2G: A pattern showing the main features and the direction of hair.

Materials for Pyrography

Pyrography is not limited to wood alone. Leather, paper, and gourds can also be used to expand and enhance the pyrographic experience. In this chapter, we look at the various considerations when burning on these and some other natural materials.

Suitable Timber

Many woods can be burned, but some are more suited to pyrography than others. Ideally, light-colored wood allows for the best contrast between the burned picture and the surface. (See **Figure 3A**.) Most people prefer wood with as little grain as possible to provide a blank canvas for burning. Heavily grained wood is more of a challenge, but if the grain is incorporated into the design, the results can be dramatic.

Dark wood can also be used, but the burned image tends to get lost in the background, especially after varnishing. For this reason, paint or other pigments are often used in conjunction with pyrography on dark materials to help the image stand out. (See **Figure 3B**.)

With a powerful enough pyrography machine, the hardest of woods can be successfully burned, but soft and evenly textured woods are more consistent to burn on and also allow the nib to make an easy impression in the wood if you wish to texture heavily.

The form of timber will largely depend on what you want to do with it. For instance, if you want to frame and hang your work you might consider

© Sue Walters

Figure 3A: *Koala.* Being blond in color, timbers like basswood allow a higher contrast between the burning and the background. Its soft, even texture also makes basswood one of the most popular of all burning materials.

© Sue Walters

Figure 3B: *Here's Looking at You.* Darker timbers provide less contrast between the burning and the background. For this reason, color is often used in conjunction to help the design stand out.

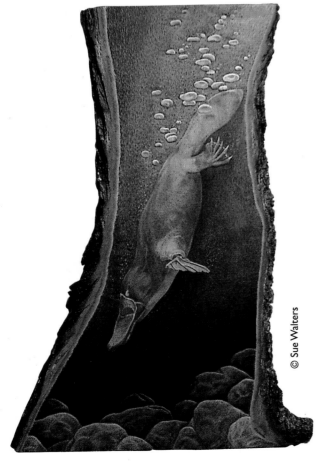

© Sue Walters

Figure 3C: *Platypus Diving.* Natural-edged timber slabs can provide a dynamic canvas for pyrography. This can be especially effective when care is taken to select a subject that suits the shape of the wood.

using plywood or veneer. Cabinet or furniture-quality plywood can make a wonderful backdrop for your work as long as you take care not to burn so heavily as to penetrate the glue layer, which lies between the sheets of timber veneer. Take the same care when using manmade wood that's been laminated with veneer.

Planks of solid timber can be found at your hardware store or timber supply store. They are excellent for signs, functional items, and wall hangings. Wood that still has its bark

TIP

Some suppliers offer a planing and sanding service.

edge left in place makes a natural and effective self-framed surface to burn. (See **Figure 3C**.) The most popular of these are the basswood rounds and planks that can be found in many craft and woodcarving stores in the United States and Canada. People in other countries might have more trouble finding this wood, so an alternative is to go to a wood supplier that specializes in exotic and natural-edged timber for the woodworking and turning community. Sometimes you can find lovely planks of natural-edged wood, which can be dressed and cut to any length you need. This is also an ideal location to shop around for burl slabs.

Wood blanks from craft stores are another popular product for pyrography. Many craft stores have a variety of products made for the folk art and pyrography industries. These blanks come in the form of untreated picture frames, kitchen utensils, boxes, plaques, and other functional items and are made from a variety of woods. In the United States and Canada, they tend to be made of basswood. In the United Kingdom, sycamore, beech, lime, and birch are popular. In Australia, pine, sassafras, and hoop pine are more common.

Another popular application of pyrography is on furniture. With some time and imagination, an inexpensive pine coffee table can be turned into a family heirloom. Even the wooden features of a house, like kitchen cabinets, can have an individual touch added to them. It's just important to remember to not burn on timber that is already treated or sealed.

Fading and Finishing

Pyrography on timber needs to be sealed for its own protection by using varnish or oil. Estapol can be used, but it does tend to yellow timber and this effect can mute the contrast of your burning. Timber stays closer to its original color when finished with acrylic varnish. For a clear, rapid-dry finish, I like to use water-based acrylic varnish or spirit-based acrylic spray on much of my own work. Tung, Danish, and other wood oils can also be used, but they do tend to darken the wood and can't be used on work that has color.

To prevent possible fading of your pyrography and the timber, varnishes containing UV inhibitors should be considered. This is especially true of work that will be exposed to strong, direct artificial or natural light. A marine varnish or a heavy-duty varnish with UV filters should be considered if the work is intended for outdoor display.

Recommended Timbers

- **Aspen:** Light colored, soft wood.
- **Basswood:** Probably the most popular burning wood. Soft, pale, and even-grained. It is similar to linden or lime in parts of Europe.
- **Beech:** Creamy colored to light brown. Fine and silky with a close, even texture.
- **Birch:** Even-grained, creamy colored wood.
- **Butternut:** Medium brown and soft.
- **Camphor laurel:** Yellowish wood, soft to medium hardness.
- **Cedar:** Light brown, heavily grained, fragrant, and soft to burn. Incorporate the grain into the work.
- **Cherry:** Light red to pink, even, tight grain.
- **Cypress:** Yellow colored and heavily grained. Incorporate the grain into the work.
- **Holly:** Very pale with little grain. Fine and even texture.
- **Hoop pine:** Soft, blond, and readily available in Australia, especially in ply. Has some broad distinctive grain but is easily managed.
- **Huon pine:** Australian timber, very pale/white wood, fine and even texture with a soft contrasting grain. Only recycled wood is permitted for use.

- **Jelutong:** Very pale and soft wood from Asia. Extremely easy to burn and provides good contrast.
- **Maple:** Cream to light brown/red, very uniform, fine grained.
- **Pine:** *Pinus radiata* and other pine can be challenging to burn. You will need to slow down while burning on the grain so you don't end up with a checkered picture. It is soft and readily available.
- **Poplar:** Very pale to yellow. Grain is medium-fine but very uniform.
- **Queensland ash:** Australian wood, pale in color.
- **Red alder:** Relatively soft wood that is pale yellow in color and evenly textured.
- **Sycamore:** Pale yellow/cream to a light honey color.
- **Yellow cedar:** Pale yellow, evenly textured.

© Sue Walters

Figure 3D: *Charging Elephant.* Being very soft and having no grain, leather is extremely easy to burn on compared to many other materials.

Materials for Pyrography

Leather

Leather is an absolute joy to burn on! It can stink a bit, but that drawback is compensated by the sheer ease of burning. (See **Figure 3D**.) There is no wood grain to negotiate or fight. The heated nib (cooler than needed for wood) sinks nicely into the surface and lets you draw with a smooth, fast rhythm that isn't always possible on wood. Leather is also quite versatile. It can be presented in a frame as something purely decorative or it can be used on functional items, such as dog collars, belts, and bags.

Leather does have a few drawbacks unfortunately. Invariably, good leather is more expensive than wood, and it can be much harder to find. I now elect to drive some distance to hand pick leather that is clean and of good quality. I can cut it up with a sharp blade and a metal ruler if the piece is large or of the wrong size. A search in the phone book or on the Internet for leather merchants would be the best start for finding a supplier. Smooth, unblemished, pale tanned leather is preferable for obvious reasons, so I suggest you go in to pick it out yourself if at all possible.

One other slight drawback is that, compared to burning on wood, leather burning can gum up and dirty your nibs very quickly. You will find yourself constantly needing to kick off built up muck as you go along. If you don't, your nib can stick and kangaroo hop across the surface, often leaving dirt deposits behind as it goes.

Naturally, cowhides are the most common leather and most readily found, but many other types of hide, including buckskin, moose, deer, and kangaroo, are suitable as long as they are vegetable-tanned and not chromium-tanned or treated with wax or oil. Many soft leathers are chromium-tanned or bleached, and the fumes caused by burning these could be harmful to your health and should be avoided. Please ask if you have any doubts.

Leather pyrography is really quite simple, but you need to remember that it requires a lot less heat to burn than timber. It's easy to irreparably damage the finished picture if care isn't taken, so keep a piece of scrap leather nearby to test your nib temperature. Most fixed-temperature, solid

point burners are cool enough to be ideal for leather burning, and variable-temperature burners can be turned down to the required gentle heat.

The aesthetic appeal of leather burning lies in its rustic, sepia appearance, but color can also be added for a subtle yet dramatic change of pace. There are several mediums that can be used to add color, but I personally prefer a thin wash of artists' oil paints suspended in turpentine. The paint is so thin that it subtly colors the leather without covering the burning. In the piece *Wedge Tail Eagle*, I burned the eagle as I normally would; then, using an oil brush, I washed a layer of yellow over the head, feathers, and eye, but not the beak. Next, I used a wash of burnt sienna and laid it over all but the tips of the feathers, leaving those yellow. A white oil wash on the beak completed the picture. (See **Figure 3E**.)

Other color pigments that can be used include leather dyes, inks, and even vegetable dye. You'll have to experiment with these to be sure they don't sit on top of your pyrography and spoil the effect. You may have to use them on untouched parts of leather only, like in folk art work. Standard acrylic paints can be used if the finished picture is to remain flat, otherwise it can flake off. Colored pencils can also be used, but, because the leather

Figure 3E: *Wedge Tail Eagle*. An embossed, almost 3D impression can easily be made in leather when burning. Color can also be used to accent the subject.

hasn't much tooth (texture to capture color), the pigment doesn't lie thick on the surface, and the effect is very subtle indeed.

The thickness of the leather isn't overly crucial, except if you plan to employ a three-dimensional effect or emboss heavily as you burn. Surface burning is easily done with any of the basic nibs, including a shader, a skew, and a writing nib.

Transfer of patterns can be done with graphite paper, but erasing is difficult so take care to cover your lines with burning. Soft lead pencils can also be used to draw designs on leather.

If your finished product will be handled often, your leather might need to be protected from dirt and moisture with a leather conditioner or leather lacquer. Even art varnish spray can be used if the piece is to remain flat and rigid.

Paper

Paper is actually quite resilient when it comes to burning. In fact, I've done some brutal things on paper with a hot pen, a blowtorch, and engraving tools, and I haven't once broken through by mistake. That's not to say that punching through won't happen if this medium is approached like woodburning. It does take a more patient and gentler approach than some other forms of pyrography, but you will find, as I did, that paper pyrography is not only very possible but also aesthetically lovely to look at. (See **Figure 3F**.)

The brilliant thing about paper burning is that you never have to spend hours searching for the perfect piece of burning wood—it's all there waiting for you at the art or craft store. It's affordable, plentiful, and easy to frame and present.

Both hot- and cold-pressed, acid-free, rag paper can be used. Cold-pressed paper has a rough texture, while hot-pressed tends to be smooth. This is the paper that watercolor artists use, and it can be bought in either single sheets or as part of a pad.

I find that smooth paper is sometimes more preferable for the beginner because its level surface is more akin to what they are used to in woodburning. Don't discount the character of rough paper, though. On textured paper, the burner tends to catch the peaks while leaving the valleys intact, and this can be used to create interesting effects or romantic/rustic moods.

© Sue Walters

Figure 3F: *Eagle Owl.* Paper burning is far more forgiving than most people expect, and the sepia effect of pyrography on paper can be quite striking.

The thickness of the paper will depend on the effect you want and your experience level. I've found that it's possible to burn on very thin paper, but this increases the chance of a hot nib punching through and it also limits how heavy-handed and textural you can be. Once the nib is in contact with the surface, the heat is readily absorbed into the paper, so believe it or not, the nib needs to be hotter than that used for wood. The trick lies in getting this hot nib down and in contact without burning a blob before the nib can cool down to its normal burning temperature. Both the runway and the blowing techniques described in chapter five will take the heat off enough to let you do this.

You could also try uncolored illustration cardboard if you really want to heavily texture and engrave the paper. It is possible to burn on colored cardboard and paper and achieve some exciting results, but for your own safety, do consider what chemicals or dyes were used to color the paper. (See **Figure 3G**.)

Materials for Pyrography

© Sue Walters

Figure 3G: *Grazing Deer.* Many different colored pigments can be used in conjunction with pyrography on paper. In this piece, an engraving tool was used to scratch grass highlights in the foreground.

You can add color to a paper burning many ways, but I prefer using watercolor, gouache, or acrylic paints. Other pigments that are normally used on paper can be used in conjunction with paper pyrography, but you should experiment first to see how they will interact with your project.

Heavy burning and paint washes can buckle paper. To help prevent this, I suggest that you stretch the paper on a board, the same way watercolor painters do. To get a detailed description of this procedure, consult a watercolor painting manual. Basically, you need to soak the paper, and then attach it to a board, so when it dries, it becomes taut. Soak the paper in clean water for about ten minutes in a bath or basin, let most of the excess water run off, then place the damp paper face up on a flat piece of thick plywood. Cut lengths of gum tape slightly longer than each side of the paper, wet them, and secure the sheet of paper to the board with the tape. Gum tape is also called gum strip and is used by watercolor artists to secure damp paper. It can be found in art stores. Thumbtacks, spaced along the edge, can also be used instead of the tape or in conjunction with tape to help fortify the join. The sheet is then left to dry.

Gourds

Gourd arts and crafts already have books, clubs, societies, shows, and magazines dedicated to them—and with good reason. Gourds are extremely versatile to use both creatively and functionally; they are unusual, unique, and popular, and they are the hot rising star of the craft industry, especially in the United States.

There is not enough room for me to go into the details of all things gourd, but they certainly do deserve a mention when it comes to pyrography, as both have been intertwined throughout history in a happy marriage of vessel and traditional design. In the past and in present day, many countries around the world use gourds as both functional and decorative objects that are often burned with basic implements, such as a metal rod heated in a fire. This relationship continues in the modern craft industry where gourd crafters

© Sue Walters

Figure 3H: *Elephant Gourd,* monochrome pyrography on gourd. Gourds are one of the most popular of all mediums to burn on. Their exotic shape and leathery appearance work beautifully with pyrography.

Figure 3I: Using a writing nib to add stippled texture to the dark background of a gourd burning. Note how the finger is planted to steady the hand.

often decorate their work with pyrography alone or in combination with other mediums. (See **Figure 3H**.)

Gourds are an inedible fruit that look similar to squash or pumpkin. When they are dry, their shell becomes hard and brown. Dried gourds can then be used and displayed in a huge variety of ways, depending on the shape and size. Containers, lamps, three-dimensional art, jewelry, masks, and birdhouses are among the many uses.

If you want to delve into the extensive world of gourds, I suggest you do an Internet search if you can. This will reap information ranging from how to grow and craft gourds to finding gourd supplies, societies, shows, and online groups. I have also included some gourd contacts in the directory in the back of this book.

The combination of gourds and pyrography lends itself beautifully to designs of natural and realistic themes, but geometric patterns and stylized subjects are also used extensively and to wonderful effect.

Gourds burn "dirty" compared to some types of wood, and the nib will need to have carbon and muck kicked or rubbed off as the work proceeds. Gourds are a little trickier to burn than flatwork because of their spherical shapes, so you will have to find a comfortable way to hold your work. (See **Figure 3I**.)

All of the usual nibs work well on gourds, but you will find that the surface of a gourd is a little shell-like and slightly more slippery to burn than soft, flat timber. This can cause an odd skid, and, for that reason, I prefer using a sharp skew to burn my lines. This knife-like nib seems to dig in and anchor itself in the surface, helping to prevent accidents and to promote a clean, crisp line.

Because the light hits at various angles, texture seems to work particularly well on gourds, so don't be afraid to experiment with patterns. You can also physically cut entire pieces out of the gourd shell with a hot nib, opening up a whole new dimension in your work. Note: It can be quite pulpy under the hard outer layer of the gourd. Have a brush and water on hand in case this area smolders when cut by a hot nib.

Color can be used in conjunction with your burning if you wish. I prefer to use acrylic paints, but many other pigments, including leather dyes and pencils, can happily be used for various effects. Again, I encourage you to experiment on scraps of material to see what best suits your style and objective.

Patterns and designs can be copied to the gourd either by traditional tracing or by graphite and heat transfer methods. A soft pencil can be used to draw on the surface, and a damp sponge can be used for erasing lines. For smooth coverage and ease, I recommend a spray varnish to seal your work.

TIP

Mini butane torches can also be used to burn broad, soft designs.

A coiled piece of cloth or a mini beanbag on your lap are various ways to hold a gourd when working on it.

After fine sanding, soak your pre-sanded tagua in three percent hydrogen peroxide for about 15 minutes. Rinse it in clean water, and then leave it to dry for a couple of days away from direct heat. This will remove a lot of oil from the burning surface. (Do not re-sand after this step or the oily surface will be re-exposed.)

Bottled 3% hydrogen peroxide can be found at your pharmacy.

Because of their size, solid nib burners are not very suitable for tagua.

If your work smells like a burnt nut after you have sealed it, add further layers until the smell stops. The smell is an indication that the pyrography is still exposed to the air and not properly sealed.

Miscellaneous Pyrographic Materials

Why not consider burning on less common natural materials such as horn, bark, or artist's conk? How about tagua, antler, ivory, or cork? Each adds a unique and exciting new challenge for the pyrographer.

Tagua

Tagua (pronounced tah-gwah) is also called palm ivory or vegetable ivory because of its similarity in look and feel to animal ivory. Tagua is actually the dried nut of the ivory palm, found growing in the Amazon Rain Forest. (Please note: tagua harvest doesn't destroy the forest. Its sustainable harvest actually helps prevent forest destruction and promotes employment.)

Because of their unique nature, tagua are sometimes difficult to locate. They can be found at some woodcarving and timber specialists as well as specialized stores. (Please see the directory for more information.) Slices can be cut from whole nuts by using a band saw, but, because of the unpredictable color and the presence of a void in the centre of most nuts, I prefer to buy individual slices from the suppliers.

Before you burn on tagua you will need to sand it smooth. Because of its hard nature, hand sanding can be time consuming. I prefer instead to use an inverted belt sander set on a slow speed.

I love tagua burning, but its high oil content makes this one of the most challenging materials I've ever used. Instead of charring or scorching the surface like other materials, you almost seem to create pictures by a combination of cooking and producing a tar-like substance.

This odd effect can make certain subjects appear quite lifelike, especially when using a sharp skew to burn the tagua. (See **Figure 3J**.) The combination of textured furrows and tar deposits caused by the sharp skew can create a very realistic looking fur effect. Simple subjects, such as a flower or a butterfly, are suitable for the beginner, but more practice is needed to master advanced projects.

Color can be used either between burned lines to add brightness or on top of pyrography to help add realism or highlights. (See **Figure 3K**.) I personally prefer acrylic paint because it sits well on top of pyrography and is vibrant and fast drying. Gouache is another good alternative, but I find traditional watercolors too transparent and oil paints unacceptable.

Figure 3J: *Lion Tagua*, monochrome pyrography on tagua. Approximately 1.5 inches high. Tagua is also called "vegetable ivory," "palm ivory," and "corozo." It can be a challenging material to burn, but the rewards can be worth it.

Figure 3K: *Wolf Head*, tagua nut, acrylic paint on top of a pyrographic burning. Approximately 1.25 inches high. Subtle color can be combined with pyrography on tagua to enhance some subject matter.

Because of the high oil content and tar production, tagua pyrography is by far the most dirty of all burning I have tried. Constant cleaning of nibs is essential to enable a smooth, clean burn. Nib selection is limited to fine nibs because the size of a tagua slice rarely exceeds 2.5 inches. I use a very fine skew for 70 percent of all of the work I do on tagua. It can be used to draw lines or to fill in and shade by using hatching, cross-hatching, and stippling (engraving by means of dots and flicks). A writing nib burns very sloppy lines, so it is often relegated to doing dots and texturing. A shading nib can be used traditionally, but it might take practice to become skilled with this nib on tagua.

To finish, I recommend spraying the work with a spirit-based acrylic. You will need to spray the surface several times to completely seal the pyrography, but not so much that you obscure the texture marks. The reason for sealing your work is because tagua burning will bleed on contact with water. It will also wear away with handling, so a decent coverage is essential to protect your work.

It's certainly challenging enough to burn in miniature without the added hassles of an oily surface and unpredictable burn, but there is no denying that people find tagua quite fascinating and that the burned nuts make terrific wearable art. (See **Figure 3L**.) If you do try tagua pyrography, please remember that it can either look very good or very bad. Don't feel discouraged if it's the latter—you won't be alone! Just try again.

Bark

The papery bark from several varieties of trees can be used for pyrography. Of the barks I have tried, both the Australian paper bark and North American paper birch require a gentle heat. I found the surface to be so soft and spongy that it was difficult for lines to hold their edge or for shading to be uniform. This created a somewhat soft, romantic effect, but it did prove a challenge for highly detailed work. It's an interesting burn, but unless you have a practiced hand, I recommend it for high contrast work or simple subjects. Silhouette is a style that can look very effective on this sort of medium.

Ivory and Bone

It is illegal to buy, sell, or trade African elephant ivory unless it is of pre-embargo stock. Generally speaking, only old piano keys and some parts of old tusk can be used for pyrography projects. Fossilized mastodon ivory can be freely bought and sold, but please check with your customs authorities about any restrictions that might apply in exporting or importing this type of ivory. Please note: it is illegal to buy, sell, or trade any Indian elephant ivory of any kind in any situation.

I can't say I've ever burned on bone, but I've talked to people who have. Based on that and my own experience on ivory, I've come to the conclusion that neither is for the faint-hearted. They both require an extremely hot nib—red hot!

TIP
Some areas prohibit the taking of paper birch, so please check with your local authorities or use private stock.

Figure 3L: *Butterfly*, acrylic paint in between pyrographic burning. Approximately 1.5 inches high. Vibrant color can be combined with pyrography in a tole-painting fashion to great effect.

Figure 3M: *Hunting Dogs*, monochrome pyrography on piano key ivory. Approximately 0.75 inches by 0.75 inches. Natural animal materials, such as bone, mastodon ivory, and piano key ivory, can provide a unique surface for miniature pyrography.

Materials for Pyrography

This heat can readily crack ivory if it is used for extended periods, so the ivory must be burned in short bursts to avoid this. I've had the most success by burning with a pointy skew, which I sometimes turn over so I can use the very tip to chink into the surface. The picture is basically made up of a series of small cuts and incised dots, something like a form of scrimshaw with heat.

My experience of ivory burning is only on piano keys so far, and, overall, I found it to be sticky, hot, and smelly, but the effect can be delicate and attractive. (See **Figure 3M**.)

Horn, Antler, and Teeth

Three other unusual materials to burn are horn, antler, and teeth. Because of my location, I've not had a chance to burn on antler or horn (and I confess I'd rather not burn on teeth), but I have seen some excellent examples of pyrography on both, especially antler. The butt end of the antler can be cut crossways to make a disc that can be turned into a pin or pendant. A light-colored area can also be sanded back on the flat surface of the antler to create an ideal canvas for a pyrographic picture. Nature scenes seem fitting and ideal for this kind of unusual platform.

Cork

Detailed burning on cork is limited because of its bumpy and soft physical makeup. Simpler designs or silhouettes seem to be better suited to this material. (See **Figure 3N**.) Make sure that you use natural cork that hasn't been treated or impregnated with any chemicals.

The finished picture can be left natural or a craft spray or varnish could be used to protect the work.

Artist's Conks (Tree Fungus)

Another highly unusual medium for pyrography is *Ganoderma applanatum*, the artist's conk. This is a plate-like fungal growth you might see protruding out from the base of a tree trunk or on a dead stump. The upper part of the plate is hard and brown, but the underneath is a creamy white color, which is the part that can be burned. If the conk is still damp, the underside is soft and very easily marked, so pick it carefully and let it dry before use. The finished piece can be sprayed with a craft varnish for protection.

© Sue Walters

Figure 3N: Because subtle detail is difficult to burn on cork, simple designs are better suited.

Varieties of Pyrography

Pyrography shouldn't necessarily be limited to using traditional burning equipment and techniques. Some of the most exciting fun can be had when we start thinking outside of the square! The following chapter shows some examples of less traditional pyrographic applications.

Negative Pyrography

Negative pyrography shows the design surrounded by dark burning so that it stands out in stark relief to its surroundings. This is achieved by using one of the following methods: adding the background or removing the picture.

Adding the Background

In this first example of negative pyrography, the outline of a design is burned, and then all areas outside the outline are colored in by burning the background. (See **Figure 4A**.) A shader is the obvious choice for burning large background areas, but other nibs can be used if you would like to add some interesting texture as well. For example, stippling, which is produced by repeatedly jabbing a writing nib into the surface to create a satiny, luxurious background, is an excellent texturing technique to use in this case.

© Sue Walters

Figure 4A: *Gum Leaves.* The black background was burned with a shading nib.

Figure 4B: A Dremel tool being used to engrave into a torch-burned background.

© Sue Walters

Figure 4C: *New York*. An example of engraving into a torch-burned background.

Removing the Picture

The other method involves completely scorching the entire surface area of the project, and then removing parts of the burned layer to reveal the natural wood color lying underneath. (See **Figure 4B**.) The initial blackening of the surface is done with either a shader or a torch. Even though it can be a dirty job, I prefer to use a torch myself. (See **Figure 4G**.) A shader tends to leave a crust on the surface, and it can also burn a little too deeply,

both of which prevent subtle removal of the layers.

A light sanding and rub down with an old rag after torching will even up patchiness and remove any loose carbon. The surface is then ready to be engraved with a blade or a rotary tool. I prefer using a handheld rotary tool with a bur or other engraving attachment.

If you wish, any wood that has been exposed by the engraving tool can then be burned using your wood-burning tool. This is an excellent way to add details to your design or to repair any engraving mistakes.

Paint can be used to add color to the engraved areas if you wish. In *New York* (See **Figure 4C**.), red, yellow, and orange paint was used to add color to the lights of the city after the engraving was completed.

Solar Burning

As most kids know, a magnifying glass combined with the sun's rays can create an effective, yet crude burning tool. There are a few adults I know of who have also tried this form of pyrography, and all advise wearing welding glasses to protect eyes from prolonged exposure to such intense light.

Obviously, with solar burning, it's not possible to get the same subtle variations as traditional pyrography, but with a steady hand (using a prop helps) and some imagination, it's possible to produce some interesting, high-contrast work.

Relief Carving

Pyrography can be used beautifully on objects that have been relief-carved or carved in the round. Bird, wildlife, and fish carvings stand out as examples of this. There are many wonderful books by expert carvers that can instruct you in this specialized pyrography. The average burner, however, can incorporate some shallow relief carving into his or her work to add interest and realism. It isn't that hard to do!

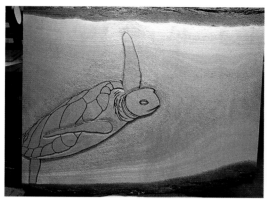

Figure 4D: A heavy-duty skew has been used to burn stop cuts along the lines to be carved up to. Some carving is done.

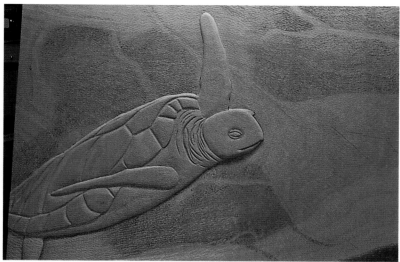

Figure 4E: The shallow-relief carving has been done and the timber smoothed.

Many pyrography machine manufacturers sell a skew that is heavy-duty enough to take the riggers of some shallow cutting. A sharp heavy-duty skew combined with high heat will cut into wood quite easily. I use this nib to burn stop cuts for pyrography projects that I also intend to relief carve.

Relief carving is simply a matter of creating a stop cut by burning and cutting on the line I intend to carve up to. The cut prevents a chisel from traveling past that line, hence the term stop cut. It should be slightly deeper than your intended carving depth. I may go over the line a few times to get it to the depth I would like, or I may burn it again after I have carved it to allow me to continue a little deeper. It is very fast, very precise, and easy to do. Then, a chisel is used to carve away any unwanted wood. (See **Figure 4D**, **Figure 4E**, and **Figure 4F**.)

Figure 4F: *Turtle Rising.* Pyrography is then added to the carving.

© Sue Walters

Torch Burning

A butane torch may be used in combination with traditional pyrography or as a burning tool on its own. Keep in mind when using this technique that the burning is a little difficult to control precisely. Torch work is most effective when it is being used to burn abstract objects, like clouds and water. Alternatively it can be used as romantic background filler or for burning decorative edging on plaques, signs, boxes, and frames. Another most interesting application of torch work is in broad abstract design. (See Figure 4G.) Gourds are also a popular canvas for torch work. Bottled gas torches and miniature burners are suitable, but I recommend the pencil variety for flexibility and ease of use.

Figure 4G: Burning an abstract design with a pencil torch.

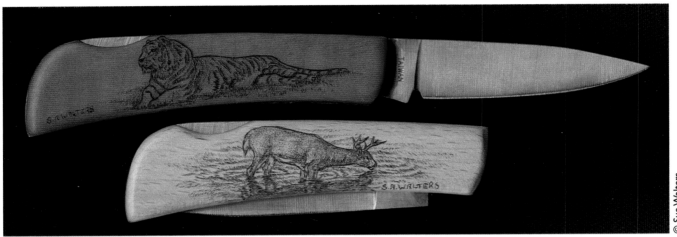

© Sue Walters

Figure 4H: Miniature pyrography on two small pocketknives.

Miniature Pyrography

Because of its tiny nature, miniature pyrography is probably one of the most difficult of all pyrographic methods to master. If you have decent eyesight and a smattering of patience, it's well worth a go because it looks wonderfully effective on small objects like knife handles and jewelry.

Nib selection is limited to the smallest of tools. A fine skew and a small, pointed writing nib are the most commonly selected. The skew is the most versatile mini-burning nib. It can be used to burn hair-thin lines and to incise tiny marks. The very tip of the skew can also be used in a scrimshaw manner, where a build up of tiny marks and dots make up the picture. (See **Figure 4H**.)

Unfortunately, because of their size, the larger solid point nibs aren't very suitable for this sort of work. Rather, variable-temperature, wire nib burners with small nibs are recommended.

Figure 4I: Pyrographic lettering.

Calligraphy

Pyrographic calligraphy can either be done freehand or by using traced lettering. It can look very effective when used for signs, plaques, inspirational words, dedications, naming, and many other things. (See **Figure 4I**.)

There are some manufacturers who supply square-shaped nibs that can be used in the same manner as traditional calligraphy pens.

For those who would prefer a guideline, the computer and printer are invaluable tools. All you have to do is type the lettering in a text program, choose the font style and size you would like to have, print out the finished product, and transfer this to your project.

This method is particularly handy if you are lettering along a curved or crooked edge. You can simply manipulate or rotate your words with the text software to reflect the angle you need.

Pokerwork

Pokerwork began with people sitting around fires and heating pokers in the coals until they were hot enough to burn wood. This type of pyrography is still practiced on many continents, often by native cultures, who use coat hangers and other metal to burn decorative designs on gourds and other objects.

If you have a yen to try this while camping out, an obvious word of caution is to be careful of the hot metal and to protect your hands.

Nib Use and Care

Pyrography is a very physical craft. At first there seems a lot to contend with, and, to some, it can seem difficult trying to burn even simple pictures. The following chapter explains the mechanics of burning and what to keep in mind to help avoid future frustration.

General Burning Guidelines

To burn a good picture, it's not necessary to bar-beque your work. Pyrography has the ability to depict an amazing range of tone and color while drawing and texturing at the same time. High heat is not required for pyrography to fulfill all of its subtle potential, but an understanding of certain basic techniques and rules is needed.

The most difficult problem newcomers face in pyrography is learning to burn consistently. Their pictures tend to look very uneven and "blobby." If this is what you are contending with, take heart. You are certainly not alone, and there are several things that can help rectify the problem.

Starting and Stopping

The first thing you need to know is that your nib will be hotter before surface contact is made than when it is actually traveling on the surface. This is because a certain amount of heat is absorbed into the material on which you are burning. How much heat is absorbed depends on what you are burning. This physical fact does bring about the most common problem that all pyrographers face at one stage or another: preventing the blob when you first make contact with the surface, before the nib cools enough to burn a consistent line.

There are two solutions to this problem. The first is motion and speed. Think of the surface of your wood as a runway. Your nib is a plane, and it is coming in to land. Just like the plane, you must be in motion when first making contact with the sur-face. This movement prevents the hot nib from sitting still in one place and burning a hole before you can get your hand moving. You can then move the nib along the surface at a speed that leaves a consistent mark. When it comes time to lift off, just like the plane, you need to continue to be in motion to prevent the nib from resting in one place—even

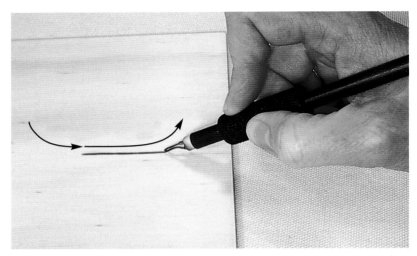

Figure 5A: To help prevent "blobbing", keep your nib in motion when touching down and lifting off.

for a split second—and burning yet another hole at the end of the line. (See **Figure 5A**.)

You might also find that just after "landing" you will need to move the nib a fraction faster for a second before all of the heat is absorbed into the material. You can then slow the nib again to a speed that burns the material consistently.

The second method to prevent blobbing is to gently blow on the nib before touchdown. This will cool the nib, and once it is on the surface and traveling, you can then stop blowing and let the burning heat return.

I know it sounds quite complex when written, but, as I've already pointed out, pyrography is a physical craft, and it needs a little patience before all of this becomes second nature.

With practice you will improve in time, trust me. You should see my early efforts! I encourage you to get some scrap material and practice "landing your plane" with the various nibs you have in your kit. Soon, the dreaded blob will be a thing of the past.

Burning Light and Dark

Once the nib is down and the heat has been absorbed, the nib will then stay at a temperature that shouldn't fluctuate if it remains in contact with the surface. Hand speed will then dictate how dark or light the line you are burning will be. Naturally, the faster you move the nib across the surface, the less time it has in contact with the material, and the lighter it will burn. The slower you travel, the darker the burning will be.

If you have a set-temperature burner, you won't be able to dial the nib temperature up or down. Nib speed will be the only way you will be able to darken or lighten your burning.

If you own a variable-temperature burner you will be able to set your dial to make the nib hotter or cooler. Temptation will exist to move the dial in tiny increments every time you want to burn a little darker or lighter, but this really isn't necessary. It is better to use the dial to get your nib at the general temperature needed to burn a given material or perform a certain technique. Once the nib heat is in that temperature range, you should then use nib speed to darken or lighten your work. For instance, if I'm burning mallee, an extremely hard wood, I will set the heat of my nib high enough to comfortably burn the wood without having the nib so hot as to nuke the surface or so cool that it doesn't show a mark. It is then up to my hand and nib speed to control how dark or light the burning will be.

It is important to note that you will need to adjust your dial for each different nib you use. A skew is made of far less metal than a shader, so it requires less to heat. If you left the setting at the same temperature as the shader, you will burn the same area far too hot.

Know the Material

The next factor in burning a consistent line is the smoothness of travel. Getting used to feeling how a nib travels on a certain surface is, once again, a matter of experience and practice. The more evenly timed your hand movement, the more even the burn will be.

Other factors also come into play as you work. Think of the surface you are burning as clothing, and think of your nib as a clothes iron. There is no way you would iron clothes with a dirty iron and not expect it to stick and hop across the surface—the same applies to pyrography. A clean, smooth nib will have far less resistance than a dirty one. The less resistance, the smoother your nib will travel. The same applies to the object you are burning. The smoother the surface of the object, the easier the nib will move across it. That is why sanding your wood nice and smooth is very important.

The next factor to consider is how much pressure to apply. This largely depends on the material you are burning and how much texture you are trying to achieve (how deep you want the nib to dig in). The harder you push, the more difficult it will be to move the nib smoothly.

The type of material you are burning also plays a part in how neat your work will be. Some timbers, like oak, are difficult to burn because of their texture, and no amount of control will help to smooth things out. Other wood, like pine, has a grain that is resinous and is difficult to burn when compared to the heartwood. When burning across grain, it pays to be patient. Slowing nib speed on dense grain areas will help to prevent your work from taking on a checkered look.

The cutting action of a skew will burn across grain better than a writing nib. Think of the grain as waves. The skew acts like the bow of a ship and cuts through the grain. In contrast, the writing nib surfs on top of the water. When it hits grain, it tends to jump over it and land heavily on the other side, making your picture look checkered and uneven.

Other Considerations

Lastly, from my experience, I have found there are a few quirky things that affect the consistency of your burning.

1) If you have your head bent too close to your work, your breath can make nib temperature fluctuate. A breeze from an open window close to your work will do the same.

2) If your nib heat starts to fluctuate (especially if your handle starts getting hot), check that all jacks and screws are tight, that the nib isn't broken or cracked, and that the handle isn't damaged. If in doubt, it's wise to consult the manufacturer.

3) Power can vary at different power points or when using extension cords and power boards. If you are having difficulties, try another point or dispense with the extension if possible.

Maintenance

I can't stress enough how important it is to keep your nibs as clean as possible. As I mentioned previously, a dirty nib will drag as it travels across the surface of your wood. This reduces the chance of an even burn and can leave unsightly dirt deposits behind in the nib's wake. It's not necessary to clean your nib after every stroke, but it is important to scrape or rub off any carbon or buildup when it occurs.

Sometimes you may notice when working (particularly on materials that create a lot of buildup), the nib will get dirty quite often. To save you from repeatedly turning off your burner, you can rub or scrape a lot of this muck off while the heat is still on. Of course, you can't use any materials that will melt when doing this.

I use a blade to clean the edge of my skew. I simply hold the blade and run it along the nib's edge. To clean a nib without having to stop work, insert the blade into a block and make your own desktop nib cleaner. (See **Figure 5B**.)

The writing and shading nibs can also be cleaned on a blade or on something slightly abrasive. You can use sandpaper, but it can wear down your nibs. I recommend using the finest sandpaper you

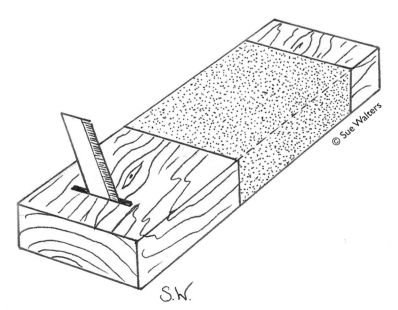

Figure 5B: A simple desktop nib cleaner is made quite easily.
1) Chisel a split into a block of wood.
2) Place a piece of blade into the split and glue it in place.
3) Glue or staple abrasive material to the block, if desired.

can find, and then sanding that paper with sandpaper. This extra sanding will take off the abrasive edge and basically leave behind a sturdy paper. This paper can then be stapled to a flat board and used now and then to rub off buildup. My cleaning board is 10 years old, black with carbon, and still works like a charm. At times I also use a piece of plain scrap printing paper or an old piece of denim to quickly rub my nibs across.

Solid point nibs are sturdier, and there is less concern about wearing them down during cleaning. The edge of a sharp blade, stainless steel scourer, or fine sandpaper can effectively clean them with the nib heat on.

When the heat is off, you can be a little more thorough with cleaning. A dry nylon pot scourer is excellent for cleaning shading, writing, and solid point nibs. I also find that flexible super-fine sanding pads clean nibs quite gently.

If you are really keen, you can polish your writing and shading nibs with a rotary tool, a felt bob, and aluminium oxide or other compound, but I confess that I haven't found the need to do this very often.

It's important to keep your skew sharp. Just like a chisel, it needs a keen edge, so now and then I use a fine sharpening stone to re-establish the edge of my skew. However, sharpening your skew too much with a stone can reduce its life. To prevent this, you can hone the edge by using a leather strop that is charged with neat's-foot oil or a fine abrasive compound. Lay the skew on its side on top of the leather at the desired angle, place your finger on the top side to support it, and gently drag the skew along the strop.

Making Your Own Nibs

If you would like to make your own nibs, you can do so by using nichrome wire. The variety of nibs that can be made is really only limited by your imagination and ingenuity, but to get you started, I will briefly describe here how I make a few of the basics.

You will need:

1) A length of nichrome wire that is long enough to make a nib to suit your burner. Measure some of your other nibs to ascertain this.

2) A firm, flat plate on which to pound the wire out. The base of an old clothes iron will do.

3) A flat-faced hammer. I use a tack hammer, which is small enough to flatten the head of the nib but not my fingers.

4) A heat source to anneal the metal before working it. Heating the metal (annealing) makes it easier to shape. You can do this by heating the wire red hot with a butane torch. You can also bend the wire into a basic nib shape and heat it as hot as your pyrography machine will allow.

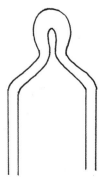

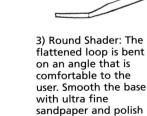
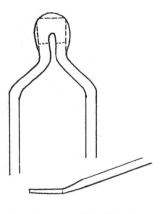

1) Writing Nib: The basic writing nib shape is formed.

2) The wire is annealed and the end of the nib is pounded flat.

3) Round Shader: The flattened loop is bent on an angle that is comfortable to the user. Smooth the base with ultra fine sandpaper and polish if desired.

4) Skew: Sand or grind off the edges of the loop as indicated. Grind or sand both sides of the flat edge to the desired angle to form a sharp edge. Hone with a stone.

5) Calligraphy Nib: Grind or sand off the edges as indicated. Bend at an angle and smooth the base with ultra fine sandpaper and polish if desired.

Figure 5C: Try creating your own nibs.

I prefer to make the basic writing nib shape before annealing, but annealing beforehand would probably work just as well. After the wire is cool and the basic writing nib is shaped, you can then pound the end of the nib with a hammer until it forms a flattened loop. This shape is the basis of making a skew, a round shader, and a calligraphy nib. (See **Figure 5C**.)

Fixing Mistakes— Sandpaper or Scraping

If a mistake is made in pyrography, it can be hard to remove, but not impossible. Most people will turn to sandpaper to erase the area affected, but I prefer scraping with a blade instead. (See **Figure 5D**.) I do this for several reasons: 1) Sanding tends to muddy and gray the area being erased, so that it looks out of place compared to the rest of the picture; 2) Using a scraper is much more precise, because a small area can be worked on without altering neighboring work; 3) The scraper will remove wood in a flat manner and not leave a sloping trench like sandpaper can; 4) The scraper can be used on all surfaces, even leather and paper; and 5) The scraper can remove a burned line without removing the wood surrounding it.

Whenever I work, I have a hobby blade next to me. It's as important to my burning kit as any other tool I use. This is what I use as a scraper if I should need to lighten an area, remove a mistake, clean up resin or tar deposit, pick out highlights, clean a nib, or sharpen a pencil.

You may like to try some sort of other blade, perhaps a stencil knife or other sharp-edged implement. Whatever you choose, you will find it's far better to gently scrape away many shallow layers than to gouge the wood by trying to remove the mistake in just a few strokes.

Even though I encourage you to try, some of you won't feel comfortable using a scraper. In that case, sandpaper is an alternative. It's very difficult to entirely remove a burned mistake by sanding, but you can often lighten the area enough to cover the original mistake with fresh pyrography.

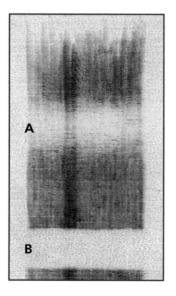

Figure 5D: I prefer using a blade to fix any mistakes because it tends to do a cleaner job than sandpaper. As you can see, the sandpaper has left a smudged area (A). The blade, on the other hand, cleanly removed the area (B).

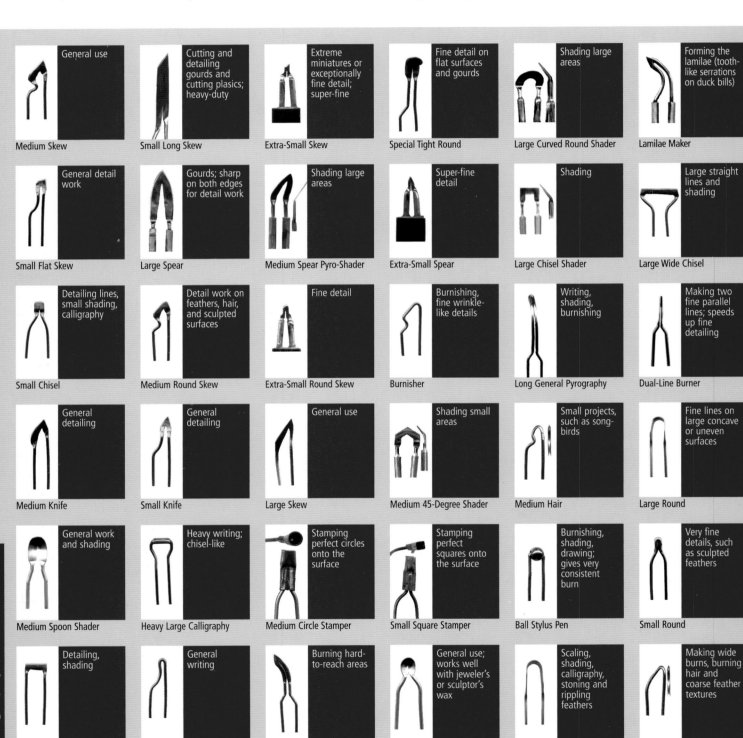

Nib Chart

Manufactured pyrography nibs can come in an enormous variety. The chart below shows a sampling of the many different nib designs available today, especially in the North American market.

Some of these nibs are specifically designed for texturing carvings, but there is no reason that they can't serve a dual purpose and be used for flat pyrography as well. Many other nibs seen here are variations of the skew, writer, and shader, and your choice of nib will often come down to personal preference.

General use — **Medium Skew**

Cutting and detailing gourds and cutting plasics; heavy-duty — **Small Long Skew**

Extreme miniatures or exceptionally fine detail; super-fine — **Extra-Small Skew**

Fine detail on flat surfaces and gourds — **Special Tight Round**

Shading large areas — **Large Curved Round Shader**

Forming the lamilae (tooth-like serrations on duck bills) — **Lamilae Maker**

General detail work — **Small Flat Skew**

Gourds; sharp on both edges for detail work — **Large Spear**

Shading large areas — **Medium Spear Pyro-Shader**

Super-fine detail — **Extra-Small Spear**

Shading — **Large Chisel Shader**

Large straight lines and shading — **Large Wide Chisel**

Detailing lines, small shading, calligraphy — **Small Chisel**

Detail work on feathers, hair, and sculpted surfaces — **Medium Round Skew**

Fine detail — **Extra-Small Round Skew**

Burnishing, fine wrinkle-like details — **Burnisher**

Writing, shading, burnishing — **Long General Pyrography**

Making two fine parallel lines; speeds up fine detailing — **Dual-Line Burner**

General detailing — **Medium Knife**

General detailing — **Small Knife**

General use — **Large Skew**

Shading small areas — **Medium 45-Degree Shader**

Small projects, such as song-birds — **Medium Hair**

Fine lines on large concave or uneven surfaces — **Large Round**

General work and shading — **Medium Spoon Shader**

Heavy writing; chisel-like — **Heavy Large Calligraphy**

Stamping perfect circles onto the surface — **Medium Circle Stamper**

Stamping perfect squares onto the surface — **Small Square Stamper**

Burnishing, shading, drawing; gives very consistent burn — **Ball Stylus Pen**

Very fine details, such as sculpted feathers — **Small Round**

Detailing, shading — **Large Chisel**

General writing — **Writing**

Burning hard-to-reach areas — **Large Curved Spear**

General use; works well with jeweler's or sculptor's wax — **Small Spoon Shader**

Scaling, shading, calligraphy, stoning and rippling feathers — **Large Versatile**

Making wide burns, burning hair and coarse feather textures — **Large Hair Tip**

The Three Basic Nibs

Nib selection is one of the least understood aspects of pyrography. Here we will examine the basic nib designs used for flat work and how they are best applied.

Selecting the Right Nib

As with any other art or craft, it's important in pyrography to select the right tool for the right job. Just as carvers learn to select a specifically shaped chisel to execute a certain cut, pyrographers must also learn that each nib will result in a different effect. This simply means that each nib has a physical shape and that this shape will govern how the nib is used, what effect will result, and what limitations it has. Using the correct nib in combination with the correct technique will greatly improve any burning.

Pyrography is like learning to drive a car. It's a very physical craft where you need to take into account nib heat, nib type, medium, speed, and pressure. It sounds like an awful lot to take in at first, but, with practice, all of this will soon become second nature.

Having said this, you can practice until the cows come home and never get anywhere unless you choose the right nib for the right job. No matter what your experience level is, you can instantly become a better burner by remembering to choose the right tool. I am going to focus on just three types of nibs—skew, writer, and shader—because I really believe they are all that is needed to perform a huge variety of burning.

Most burning kits will have variations of the skew, writer, and shader. They may be given different names and may look slightly different, but generally you will find that they fall into three distinct shape types. 1) Skew: This nib will have a straight edge and is best for burning or cutting crisp, neat lines. 2) Writer: This nib culminates in a round point and is best used for lettering, curved lines, and filling in. 3) Shader: This nib will generally appear flat and is designed to "iron" the surface, leaving a soft, wide scorch mark. Let's look at each basic nib and see what function it performs.

Wire Nib Skew

Solid Point Skew

Figure 6A

The Skew

The skew has a straight, often knifelike edge. (See **Figure 6A**.) Its narrow edge gives it the ability to burn very fine, crisp, and precise lines. It's designed to etch as it burns and is excellent for burning straight or lazy curved lines, but it is limited when burning tightly curved lines. It is also limited to filling in areas by crosshatching and other similar methods.

How to Use the Skew

The skew works best pulled toward the body. (See **Figure 6B**.) For this reason, you will need to keep turning your work so that the nib can continue to generally travel toward you. For a straight line, you simply have to draw the nib straight back toward yourself. For short lines and areas where you require good control, it's better to use your little finger to steady the hand. When doing long lines, your hand can be clear of the surface to allow for unobstructed traveling of the nib for the distance required.

You will find you need to "roll" your fingers from side to side (as indicated by the arrows) to burn curved lines, much like a skater does with skate blades when turning on ice.

The skew is best kept very clean and sharply honed for optimal performance.

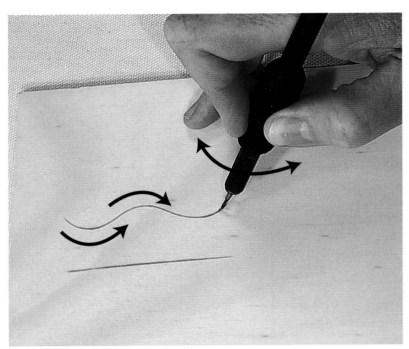

Figure 6B: The skew is best pulled toward yourself. A slight twisting motion with your fingers will allow gentle curved lines to be burned.

Practice
- Practice burning light and dark lines with the aim of producing a line of uniform darkness.
- Slow down and speed up your hand movement to see how this influences the color. Keep in mind the runway landing and take-off technique to eliminate blobbing at the beginning and end of the stroke.
- Try burning deep and shallow to see what effect it produces.
- Burn parallel lines close to each other to learn directional control.
- Practice rolling your fingers and burning increasingly tighter curved lines.

Suggested Uses: Skew

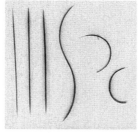

Line
The skew is capable of burning extremely fine, crisp lines. Wire nib skews can be extremely sharp and can cut as they burn, which is excellent for texturing fur, for example. It burns across grain more efficiently than a writing nib because it cuts through the grain rather than jumping over it. It's especially suited for edging, wildlife, miniature, and linear work.

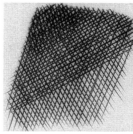

Fill/Shading
Because of its thin edge, the skew is limited in how it can shade or fill in work. Crosshatch is a method of shading by crossing a series of parallel lines. The tighter the lines and the more times they cross, the darker the area. Skews are perfect for this kind of work.

Fill/Shading
Hatching is another method where the skew can be used to create a darker area. The closer together the lines are, the darker the area is. Care must be taken to not get the line too close to its neighbor, in case the lines merge.

Fill/Shading
The edge of a skew can be tapped against the surface in a random, overlapping manner. This method is much like stippling with a writing nib. The more layers of cuts you add, the darker the area will become. This technique could be used for very subtle shading or a soft background.

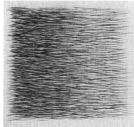

Fill/Shading
Short or long lines running in the same direction but slightly askew to each other can create subtle shading or filling. It is especially effective when used to represent animal fur.

Lettering
Lettering with a skew is generally limited to the edging of larger letters. Because the blade is sunk slightly into the surface you are burning, it is awkward to turn very tight curves, making small lettering and characters like "O" difficult to burn. The skew is an excellent nib to edge lettering for a sign.

Wire Nib Writer, North American style

Solid Nib Writer

Figure 6C

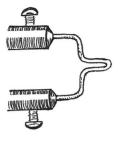

Wire Nib Writer, European/Australian style

The Writer

The writer, like a pencil, has a pointed or rounded end, which allows it to go in any direction while in contact with the surface. (See **Figure 6C**.) This makes it ideal for writing or burning tight curves and circles. It can be used to fill in and shade areas, although this can take some time and look grainy.

Figure 6D: The writing nib can travel in any direction.

How to Use the Writer

When burning with this nib, the hand can rest on the surface in a typical writing position. Because it floats on the surface (compared to a skew, which cuts through the wood), this nib can travel in any direction. You will, however, find it more comfortable to run the writer toward you when doing most lines, so it's best to keep turning your work to allow your nib to keep moving in a comfortable direction. (See **Figure 6D**.)

Practice

- The writing nib is the main culprit when it comes to the dreaded blob, so it's essential to practice runway landing and takeoffs to eliminate this problem.
- When your nib is down, try to keep the speed even to produce uniform color. Vary your hand speed to see the effect.
- If lines appear uneven, practice going back over them to smooth out the inconsistency. (Notice how the writer burns better with the grain than across it.)
- Try writing your name without turning the work to learn how to burn away from yourself.
- Burn circles and curves.
- Lastly, experiment. Fill in areas with continuous squiggles, stipple, and generally see what it can do.

Suggested Uses: Writer

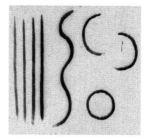

Line
Because the writer has a fatter edge than the skew, it will burn a wider, softer line. This also means that the writer tends to sit on top of the surface, so it takes a little more control to burn a neat line. This feature makes the writer the ideal nib for difficult curves, soft lines, the eyes of animals, lettering, and filling in small areas.

Fill/Shading
Because the writer is essentially a point touching the surface area, you are limited to how you can fill or shade an area. The only way to do this is to overlap certain patterns. In this sample, parallel lines are laid next to and on top of each other. The darkness is dictated by laying more lines or by burning each line darker.

Fill/Shading
One of the most underrated pyrography techniques is stippling. This is a method of using only dots to build up a picture (also called pointillism). It is very time-consuming, but the effect is worth the effort, plus it's very difficult to make mistakes. The more dots, the darker the area.

Fill/Shading
Squiggling the writing nib repeatedly over the surface in random, overlapping circles will also fill an area nicely. The trick is to keep the nib constantly moving and to lay the squiggles at random. It's also better to build darkness by adding subsequent layers than to try to darken an area all at once.

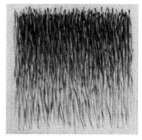

Fill/Shading
Short or long lines running in the same direction but slightly askew to each other can create subtle shading or filling. It is especially effective when used to represent animal fur. Refer to "Suggested Uses: Skew" and note how much softer the fur looks when done with a writing nib as compared to a skew.

Lettering
As the name suggests, this writing nib excels in lettering. It is able to burn the tightest of curves, making it possible to smoothly burn the difficult letters.

Wire Nib Flat Shader

Trowel-Shaped Solid Point Shader

Solid Point Shader

Figure 6E

Figure 6F: The shading nib can be pulled toward yourself...

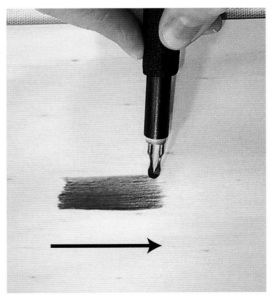

Figure 6G: ... or it can be swept sideways.

The Shader

The shader can come in many shapes and sizes, but essentially it is designed to scorch larger areas of wood or other material. (See **Figure 6E**.) It is especially good for gradient tones, shading, and filling in. The two main types of shader are the flat shader and the spoon shader.

The base of the shader is very good for filling in black areas, such as on signage or in the background of a picture. Gentle overlapping of layers can also produce soft gradient tones, such as those used in portraits; but keep in mind that this is one of the more difficult techniques and that it will take some time and practice to master. (See the Gradual Tone section in Chapter 9.) The toe of the shader can be used to draw thinner lines or to texture. It is also the ideal nib to use to heat transfer a pattern.

How to Use the Shader

Depending on the shape of your shader, there are generally two ways to use it. One way is to draw the shader back toward yourself. (See **Figure 6F**.) You will find that this movement will shorten your stroke compared to the longer sweeping motion of moving your hand sideways. (See **Figure 6G**.) I also find it much easier to develop an even rhythm for consistent overlapping of lines when I use a sideways hand motion.

Practice

As seen in the pictures to the left, repeated overlapping of shading lines can produce subtle changes of tone. Consistency of speed and smoothness of stroke is essential in this technique.

- Practice burning lines of even color, always keeping in mind the runway landing and take off so you are not left with a darker beginning or end. Keep the speed along the line even.
- Try to develop a rhythm: burn one line, lift off, and immediately swing around to lay another line next to the last.
- Go back over patchy areas with quick, light strokes to try to fill in any gaps.
- Practice building up gradual tone by first laying a light coverage, and then adding subsequent layers so that you have a smooth scale ranging from light to dark.
- Lastly, go crazy with your shader and use it in as many ways as you can. Try drawing and shading with the toe, shade by circling the nib over the surface, push it in, and see what patterns it produces.

Suggested Uses: Flat Shader

Line
The line of the flat shader will be as wide as the plate that is in contact with the surface. This will produce a broad, hard-edged line. A sweeping curve is possible, but tight curves are generally not, unless you are burning with the toe of the nib.

Fill/Shading
Repeated overlapping of the thick lines can create fill or shading. It's better to gradually build up the layers to get a smooth transition in color. Bad technique or lack of practice might lead to unsightly darker lines where each stroke covers the next. A spoon shader might be considered if this is the case.

Fill/Shading
The plate of the flat shader can also be pushed repeatedly into the surface in an overlapping, random manner. It is obviously a much less precise way of covering an area than stippling with a writing nib, but is a worthwhile method for soft focus work or for darkening a background.

Fill/Shading
Squiggling the shader repeatedly over the surface in a random manner will create overlapping circles that will also fill an area nicely. The trick is to keep the nib moving to avoid laying the squiggles in lines. It's also better to build darkness by adding subsequent layers than to try to darken an area all at once.

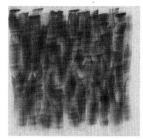

Fill/Shading
Short or long lines running in the same direction but slightly askew to each other can create shading or filling. This technique could be used when representing coarse animal fur. It could also be used for filling in lettering, for texture, or for darkening a background.

Lettering
Flat shaders can be used to burn bold lettering. Some pyrography supply companies actually offer a nib especially designed for calligraphy writing. The size of your shading nib will dictate how small you can burn lettering.

Figure 6H: Wire Nib Spoon Shader

The Spoon Shader

It's no surprise that the spoon shader is shaped like a spoon. (See **Figure 6H**.) Its base covers less area than a flat shader, but, because it has no hard edges, there is less chance of developing dark, overlapping lines when burning gradient tone. This makes it ideal for soft, gradient, tonal work but less ideal for mass filling in of large areas.

If you think of the spoon shader as a fat pencil, you will see that it's capable of being pushed in multiple directions. This makes it ideal for soft-effect stippling and also filling in by moving it in a circular motion. (See **Figure 6I**.) also use the toe of the spoon shader extensively to shade and fill in tight spaces.

Figure 6I: The spoon shader is ideal for soft-effect stippling.

Practice

Good shading and gradual tone are considered the most difficult of strokes to master in pyrography, so like using the flat shader, practice will be rewarded with better results.

- Practice gradient tone just as you would with a flat shader.
- Tip the spoon up slightly and try burning soft lines with the toe. The toe is excellent for burning soft, fat lines that have no hard edge. This makes it ideal for shading in tight areas or filling in gaps in streaky shading.
- Lastly, as I recommend with all of your nibs, experiment with your spoon shader. Squiggle it in circles, stipple, and play with it to see what its capabilities are.

Suggested Uses: Spoon Shader

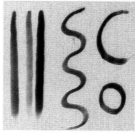

Line
The line of the spoon shader is soft because of its lack of a hard edge. Because it can be pushed and pulled in any direction, it is capable of burning fat circles and curved lines.

Fill/Shading
Repeated overlapping of the soft lines can create fill or shading. To achieve a subtle change of color, it is best to gradually build the tone by burning layer upon layer with a sweeping, even motion. This is often used to convey smooth objects such as the human form, water, an apple, or the nose of an animal.

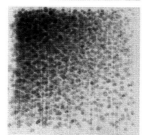

Fill/Shading
Stippling with a spoon shader creates a soft, out-of-focus effect when compared to using a writing nib. The effect is achieved by tapping the bowl on the surface in an overlapping, random pattern. For a subtle gradient, it is best to build layers rather than try to fill an area all at once. The more dots there are, the darker the area. Excellent for backgrounds and fuzzy fur.

Fill/Shading
Circling the spoon shader repeatedly over the surface in a random manner creates overlapping circles that will also fill an area nicely. The effect of this will be more soft and romantic than when done with the writing nib. It's better to build darkness by adding subsequent layers than to try to darken an area all at once.

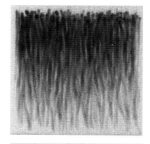

Fill/Shading
Short or long lines running in the same direction but slightly askew to each other can create subtle shading or filling. It is especially effective when used to represent animal fur. The effect of this is much softer than when done with a writing nib.

Lettering
The spoon shader will produce soft lettering that has no hard edges. Because it can be pushed in any direction it is capable of burning the difficult letters such as "O."

Texturing

When you open up your mind to the possibility of using texture in your pyrographic work, you open up a whole new world of possibilities. In this chapter, we look at creating texture and patterns and their use in adding realism and interest to your burning.

The Basics of Creating Texture

A pyrography tool is far more than a hot pencil. A pencil can only sit on the surface of the material upon which you are drawing; a burner can do so much more. Yes, it can be used to draw on the surface, but you are missing out on one of the best aspects of pyrography if you exclusively do so.

Most people starting out in burning understandably think pyrography is basically about drawing hot lines or scorching the surface of timber. Many don't realize that their burner is capable of etching and carving many textures, textures that can greatly enhance their work by giving it a more realistic, three-dimensional appearance. Not only this, but by using your nib as a branding iron and pressing it into the surface, you can create endless combinations of wonderful patterns.

Even the most basic of wire nib burners can be used in a variety of interesting ways. Remember, the writing nib of the wire tool is simply a bent piece of wire, but as you can see on the following texture chart, no less than 24 of these squares were made by this one simple nib. With a little imagination, a writing nib has become so much more.

Of course, this thought can be carried over to any nibs you might have in your kit. The standard kits for most burning tools usually have three basic nib designs: the knife-shaped skew, the pointy-shaped writer, and the broad, flat shader. With this in mind, I have completed the texture chart in this chapter using just those three nib shapes. Some kits also contain a fat bullet-shaped or spoon-shaped shader, and, since I'm a fan of the spoon shader, I thought I'd use this on a few squares as well. Looking at the texture chart, you can see that each small patch of repetitive strokes has not only given a square an individual texture, but also its own unique look and color.

Repetitive patterns don't necessarily have to be used as part of a picture. Sometimes they can be used in the background to frame or highlight the design in the foreground. In **Figure 7A**, you can see how the tip of a hot writing nib has been repeatedly pushed into the background to form a stippled mat. Not only does it provide a dark backdrop to accent the Celtic design, but the texture also creates interest and a contrast to the smooth wood. (See Square 1G on page 54.)

The use of a repetitive pattern can also create interesting textures that closely resemble those found in nature. For example, note how Square 5B looks like moonlight reflected off water and how Square 2D looks just like the fur of an animal.

Figure 7B shows a burning of an elephant's eye. What looks like a very complex picture is actually a gradual buildup of a broad, stippled pattern created by a spoon shader. While a shader is perfect for reproducing the smooth texture of an apple, that same shader, used in a different manner, can also burn an effective hide or reptile skin. It's an excellent example of how nature can be reproduced by pyrography using patterns and combinations of strokes.

You might now be wondering when you are supposed to push your nib in and when you're not. This will largely depend on what you are drawing or what effect you're trying to achieve, but let's not worry about that for now. That will be covered in more detail later in the book. All you have to do at the moment is have some fun by making up your own texture chart using the nibs you have on hand. It's a terrific way for you to not only learn the capability of each of your nibs, but also start learning about texture. I encourage you to play around as much as you can; vary your heat (if you have a variable-temperature burner), turn your nib every which way, and try whatever comes to mind. It's great practice for your hand control, and I'll guarantee you'll learn quite a bit in the process.

Draw up some one-inch by one-inch squares with a 2B pencil and a ruler on some soft, pale wood. Gather your nibs together and then go to town making as many textures and patterns as you can. (See **Figure 7C.**) When you've finished your tapestry you can hang it up on the wall as a handy pyrographic reference. It's a good idea to have a corresponding sheet of paper ready to note how each square was made.

Remember, all of the squares I have done were created with just four nibs! Given more time, a

Figure 7A: Stippling the background with a writer creates a satiny appearance on this basswood piece.

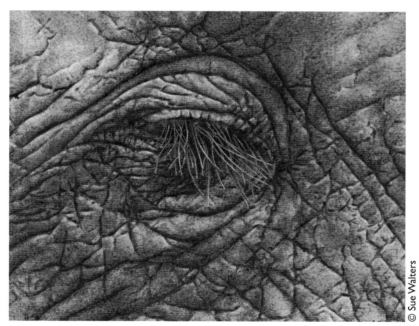

Figure 7B: *Elephant Eye*, almost entirely burned by stippling a pattern of dots. Birch ply.

few more pages, and a challenge to my imagination, I could have kept going. This goes to show you how much can be done with just a few nibs. As with most things in art and craft, it's not how much you have, but how well you use it. For example, *Elephant Eye* was done with just two nibs: a skew and a spoon shader.

TIP

Let the heat work for you. Don't damage your nib by pushing it too hard.

Texturing

53

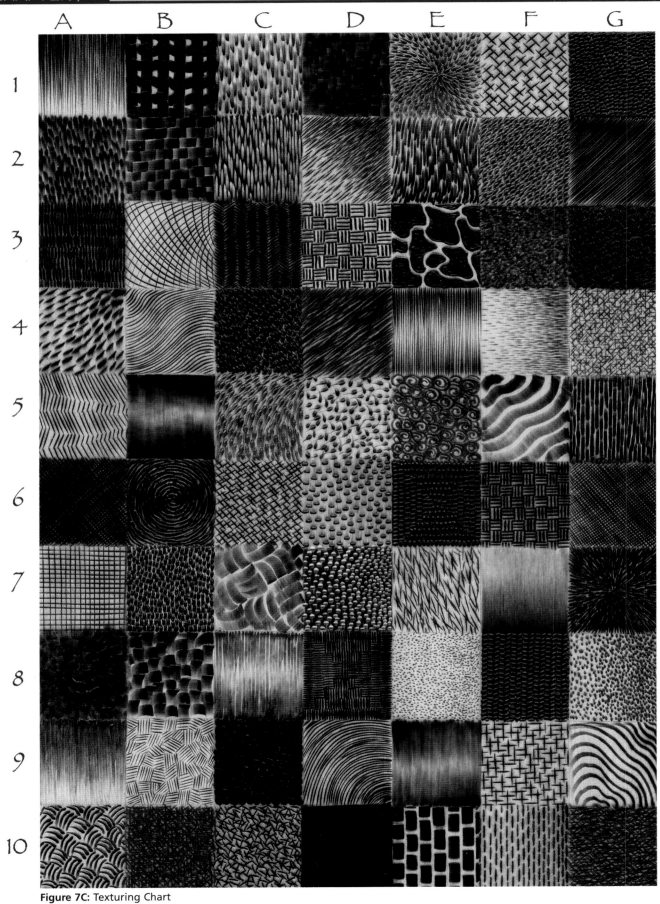

Figure 7C: Texturing Chart

	A	B	C	D	E	F	G
1	**Skew:** dragged top to bottom; allowed to trail off	**Flat shader:** crossed in wavy lines	**Writing nib:** short, random, staggered dashes, one direction	**Flat shader:** short strokes randomly overlapped	**Writing nib:** short flicks radiating out from the center	**Skew:** pushed in: crossed at random right angles	**Writing nib:** pushed in, tightly abutting each other
2	**Spoon shader:** tip of the nib, short flicks in one direction	**Flat shader:** short strokes trailing off; checker pattern	**Writing nib:** coolish, deep strokes, surface then burnt with shader	**Skew:** pushed in randomly, one direction, more strokes in the darker area	**Writing nib:** random strokes trailing off, wavy pattern	**Writing nib:** very short flicks in tight random pattern, one direction	**Skew:** lines drawn close side-by-side in one direction
3	**Flat shader:** toe pushed in, row-next-to-row pattern	**Skew:** lines arced and crossed	**Skew:** pushed in, herringbone pattern	**Writing nib:** drawn in neat basket weave pattern	**Shader or writer:** Interlocking random patterns	**Writing nib:** tight, circular, overlapping random pattern	**Flat shader:** very hot, pushed in, random cross pattern
4	**Flat shader:** toe pushed in and flicked	**Skew:** lines drawn in tight wavy pattern	**Writing nib:** side of a writing nib pushed in; random, tight pattern	**Skew:** hot, random slashes, one direction	**Skew:** parallel lines drawn from opposite sides toward the center	**Skew:** short flicks in one direction, darker area has more flicks	**Skew:** fine, random flicks at cross angles
5	**Skew:** straight, angled lines drawn parallel to each other	**Flat shader:** pulled from opposite sides towards the middle	**Writing nib:** short flicks arcing in a similar direction	**Writing nib:** jabbed in and flicked to form a tail	**Writing nib:** tight spirals slightly overlapping each other	**Flat shader:** wavy lines next to each other	**Writing nib:** deep strokes, one direction, peaks scratched off with blade
6	**Skew:** close, parallel, hot lines at cross angles	**Writing nib:** short strokes next to each other in spiral pattern, center out	**Skew:** toe pushed in tight, random pattern at cross angles	**Writing nib:** open stippled pattern, shading added on top	**Writing nib:** rows pushed in with writing nib, turn the board for next row	**Flat shader:** toe pushed in, basket weave pattern	**Skew:** very fine lines at cross angles
7	**Skew:** lines crossed at right angles	**Writing nib:** very hot, pushed in deeply, peaks then scratched off with blade	**Flat shader:** curved basket weave pattern	**Writing nib:** coolish; pushed in deeply; surface burnt with shader	**Skew:** full length pushed in, shallow cross angles	**Spoon shader:** several layers to build gradual tone	**Flat shader:** jabbed in, radiating from center outward
8	**Flat shader:** short strokes radiating from the center out	**Flat shader:** short strokes flicked down and then across	**Writing nib:** parallel lines drawn from opposite sides toward the center	**Flat shader:** toe pushed in lines, rotate board for each line	**Skew:** very tip, random stippling	**Writing nib:** pushed in, herringbone pattern	**Writing nib:** dotted on surface; more dots make a darker appearance
9	**Writing nib:** pulled from top to bottom and allowed to trail off	**Skew:** lines in blocks angled and adjacent to each other	**Spoon shader:** bowl pressed into the surface in overlapping stipple	**Skew:** lines in a sloppy quarter circle	**Spoon shader:** parallel lines drawn from opposite sides towards the center	**Skew:** pushed in; random right-angled pattern	**Spoon shader:** toe pushed in, lines drawn in wavy pattern
10	**Writing nib:** lines drawn in curved basket weave pattern	**Skew:** pushed in at both right and cross angles	**Spoon shader:** turned over, tip pushed in at various angles	**Spoon shader:** full, smooth cover	**Flat shader:** brick pattern	**Flat shader:** tip pushed in, brick pattern	**Skew:** long strokes overlapping at various angles

Figure 7C: Texturing Chart

Ducks and Bulrushes: A Beginner's Project

© Sue Walters

When considering their first project, most pyrographers ask the same question: "How do I know which nib to use on what part?"

This beginner's project will introduce you to the basic use of the skew, the shader, and the writing nib as they are used in composing a picture.

Introduction

As I have already written, you can do an awful lot of pyrography using just the basic three nibs: the skew, the shader, and the writing nib. Yes, there are many other varieties of nibs on the market as well, but you will find that a great deal of these are variants or descendents of these three. Other nibs tend to be designed as texturing tools for use in the woodcarving industry.

When it comes to nib choice in constructing a picture, there are really only two things to consider: 1) what this particular nib is physically able to do, and 2) the object that you are physically trying to portray. I know this might sound a little too general for a pyrographer grappling with the nib issue, so let me explain further.

As we see in Chapter 6: The Three Basic Nibs and in Chapter 7: Texturing, each of the basic nibs will leave a distinct impression on the wood depending on the physical makeup of the nib and the various ways it can be stroked or pushed. This holds true of any other nib design as well. Each nib leaves a certain physical impression on the surface, depending on its physical profile. The trick is to match the physical capability of the nib to the object that you are trying to portray.

For instance, a skew leaves a clean, sharp impression, so it is the ideal nib to create a crisp line. In nature, reeds have crisp outlines, therefore I selected the skew to burn their outer edges in this project. The same principle applies to the water. In nature, the physical appearance of water is soft and smooth, therefore, I chose a shader to convey this smoothness.

Before We Begin

To the beginner, I can't stress enough how vitally important it is to practice. Neat pyrography really is a matter of consistent speed and pressure. It is only the very few who pick up a pyrography pen for the first time and manage to burn neat lines. For the rest of us, our first pictures seem to be a series of blobby, impressionistic images. Take heart if you are in this category: this is the rule rather than the exception, and only practice will smooth out any inconsistencies you encounter.

It is also important that you have a practice board of scrap material at hand. This material should be identical to your main project. It can be used to practice strokes or, if you have a variable temperature burner, to test the heat of the nib. If you have a set temperature burner, you can only adjust the intensity of burning by moving your hand more or less rapidly.

Practice burning a long and consistent line with your skew. Try to get the nib heat at a temperature that burns a dark line as you move your hand at a comfortable speed. If you find that the line has flared or is far too dark, increase your nib speed or turn the heat down a little more. If you find that the line is dark in some places but light in others, try to focus on keeping your nib moving at a consistent speed.

Practice filling areas with your shader. Try burning several slightly overlapping lines next to each other. Go back over these joined lines and try to add another layer of lines on top. Blend the two areas together at the edge by dragging the edges of the dark area just slightly into the lighter area. (Please see Chapter Nine: Gradual Tone for further details.)

The Components

In this section, we'll discuss the techniques for the various components. Later on, we'll look at the steps for the entire piece in the Coming to Life section.

This beginner's project is made up of three basic components: the bulrushes, the ducks, and the water. In the various stages, we'll discuss what nib is best used and how best to use it.

The Bulrushes

The bulrushes look complicated, but they really aren't. When broken down, the straps are simply two crossing lazy S's, and the rushes are a set of parallel lines. Shading is then added to give a more realistic effect. Shading helps to show the shape has form and also from which direction the light shines.

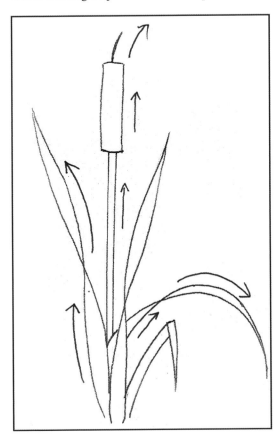

1 Outline the rushes with a skew. A skew has a knife-like edge, so it is best used to portray the crisp outer edge of the reeds and straight edges of the rushes. (Option: a writing nib can also be used, but it will burn a fatter, softer line.) Practice on some scrap material to get your nib at a temperature that will burn a neat, dark line at a speed with which you are comfortable. In time, you will find yourself more confident, and you will want to burn faster. When this happens, turn the heat up to compensate for the increased speed.

The strap reeds themselves are two intersecting curved lines. Because it looks more natural to taper the leaves off at the end, it's a good idea to turn your board upside down and burn from the base up. Follow the direction of the arrow for the entire length of the line, lifting your nib off the board at the end in a rapid flicking motion to allow the line to taper away. Burn its partner line in the same manner, but don't stop at the intersecting lines; simply cross over the other line and keep going until they join at the end. A turning motion of your fingers will allow you to gently angle the skew to follow the curved lines, much like a skater does on ice.

The stalks and rushes are two sets of parallel lines. When burning a long line, it is better to lift your hand off the surface and move your forearm in a long fluid motion. Note that the tops and bottoms of each rush are curved to give the impression of a cylinder. For the tail of the rush, burn the base slowly and then flick the nib off the surface to allow the line to trail off.

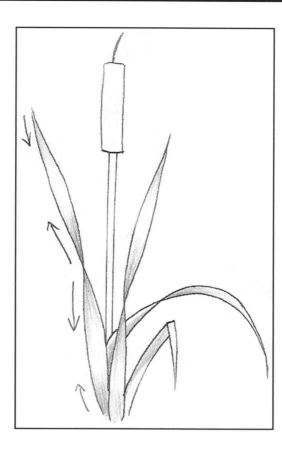

2 The shading on the reeds is an excellent way to add a realistic effect to the twisting of the strap leaves. Because shading isn't a tangible structure, we are going to use a shader to convey the soft, gentle tones.

We want this shading to be subtle and in control, so, if you can, adjust the heat of the nib so that it burns the surface gently. You can always turn it up a little more if it's not quite hot enough.

Start at the crossover point of each intersecting line and pull the shader outward from that point in a fluid stroke, allowing it to trail off. You might find that you have to overlap a few of these lines to cover an area. If you find you have left a line of shading too short, go back to the crossover point and redo the line to its correct length. It looks more natural to stagger where the lines trail off rather than leave them in a straight line. (Option: you can also burn a series of soft, overlapping lines with a writing nib to get a similar effect.) To pull your shader toward you in a fluid stroke, you will have to turn your board whichever way is necessary.

3 When filling in the seed heads, you are trying to do two things: 1) give the rushes texture and 2) create an illusion that they are round in shape by shading the outer edges of the heads. There are two methods of burning the seed head. The seed head on the left is stippled, and the seed head on the right is textured with soft, horizontal lines.

The stippled effect is created by building up overlapping dots that are made by tapping the round point of a writing nib into the surface. This can be done in three layers. First, turn the heat down and cover the entire area in light dots. Next, turn the heat up slightly and re-stipple all but the center third. Lastly, turn the heat up slightly again and stipple only the outer edge to make it darkest.

Use a writing nib to create the other seed head. Start at the outer edge of each rush and pull a short line toward the center, but allow it to trail off before it gets to the halfway point. Repeat this all the way down the head, slightly staggering the ends of each line.

To add an extra touch of realism, as indicated by the arrows, you can use the shader to add a shade line where the leaves overlap.

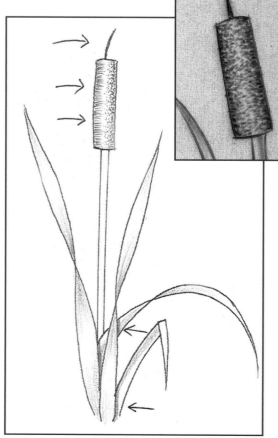

This photo shows a detail of the two methods for filling in the seed heads.

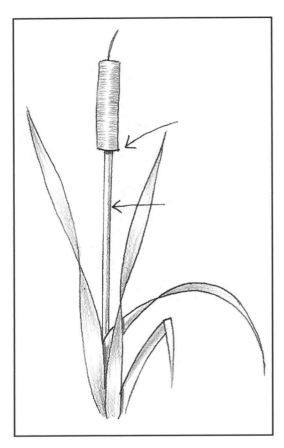

4 Lastly, use the shader to add a line of shading to the side of each stalk. This shading should be placed on the side opposite the direction of the sun. Add a touch of shading on the stalk, below the seed head. (See inset in Step 3.)

5 By adding a different seed head, you can make strap leaves burnt in this manner look like broadleafed grass or wheat. These seed heads were simply created by burning skew lines in decreasing lengths.

The Water

Water can be as simple or as complex as you choose to make it. A few simple sweeps of a shader will produce the illusion of water with little effort. More complex water is a little more difficult to unlock, but, in reality, it is simply a collection of abstract tonal patterns.

In this project, you may wish to keep it simple and go no further than Step 2, or you can experiment and complete all of the stages that follow.

1 When I make a pattern of water, I overlay the reference with a piece of tracing paper and trace lines around and along the very darkest sections. It's a good idea to lighten the pattern lines after they are transferred to the wood so that they don't show through the thin layers of tone that will be burned on top.

2 Water is smooth, so the ideal nib to represent it is the shader. The shader will allow you to burn sweeping areas of soft tone that can be blended together. Here I have begun filling in the dark areas of the water, as indicated by my pattern lines. As you can see, even at this stage, the effect is quite realistic. You can stop here if you wish, or continue with the steps below.

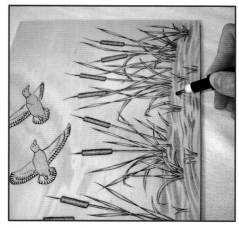

3 You may find it easier to turn your work sideways to burn large tonal areas such as water. This allows your hand to move across the work in a broad, sweeping manner.

4 If you look closely at water, you will see it has interlocking tonal sections of dark, medium, and bright white. To add a little more depth to the water, I now burn blended patches of dark over some parts of the areas I already worked.

It is important that you adjust your heat to be able to add blushes of tone in a subtle way. The burner should not be so hot that it burns dark, distinctive patches that stand out and are difficult to blend with the area below. To help blend and marry the two tonal layers together, use the shader to trail off the edges of any additional burning.

5 Mid-Tones: The very brightest (white) areas of the water will remain unburnt. All that remains to be burnt are any mid-tone areas—the color of the water between the darkest and the lightest areas. A cooler burner is needed for this step to enable you to gently merge the areas of dark together while leaving the areas of sun reflection unburnt.

Lastly, don't forget that you can use the edge of a blade to scrape out some highlights or to repair any areas that were burned too darkly. (Please see the Blade Use section in Chapter 9 on page 69.)

The Ducks

To burn the ducks, we will use all three of the basic nibs. We will also be adding a little bit of texture to their bodies to add another touch of realism.

1 Because the ducks' bodies have straight edges, we will mostly use a skew to outline them. In some areas, like the loops at the end of the feathers, a skew will not be able to form the tight curves. For these areas, we can use a writing nib to burn the outline.

Use a skew to burn short, crisp lines to define each feather. Also use the writing nib to burn the beak and a dot for the eye.

2 To define the feathers further, use a writing nib or the toe of a shading nib to burn a soft, dark line below each sharp skew line. Use the same nib to burn a looping band on the tail of each bird.

To add a little bit of texture to the bodies, use a writing nib and cover the entire area in tiny, overlapping circles. Keep the tip of the writing nib constantly moving and don't lay the squiggles in lines. The tighter the circles are, the smoother the texture will appear.

Keep the color of this first coverage quite light. We want to add the lightest of colors while creating the basis of texture. Soon we will add subsequent layers. (This same method is used to create a rough rock in Chapter 10.) Finally, add some definition to the heads and bills of the birds by burning just a little bit of color on the faces where indicated.

3 Here the bodies are going to be filled out by adding two additional layers of squiggles. Add another layer of circles on top of the area already burned, leaving alone those areas to which you don't want to add any more color. For the darkest areas, like those on the chest, another layer of squiggles is added on top.

In this method, it is better to build each layer subtly on top of the other rather than trying to add all of the darkest areas at once. This technique creates a gentle build up of the layers, allowing them to blend together more easily and to give a greater feeling of depth.

4 Lastly the edges of the wings are colored. We only want a blush of smooth color here, so a shading nib is perfect. On the outer row of each wing, burn a medium tone from the outer edge in. On the next row, do the same, but this time turn the burner down a little so that this area is a little lighter, giving the wing a staggered effect of a dark outer row and a lighter inner row. The same blush of darkness can be given to the tail, from the dark bar inward.

Add a tiny blush of extra darkness to each bird's head just behind the bill and under the neck. Further define the wings by using the shader to burn a soft patch of tone where indicated.

1 Step One: Outlining

Outlining the project defines all of the areas to be filled in. The water isn't outlined because it has no edges. Note: more heavily grained timber can be used for landscapes such as this. Figured wood is perfect to help suggest a cloudy sky or water.

2 Step Two: Filling In

Once the outlining is complete, the filling in can begin. At this stage, the reeds have been completed, the dark line below each feather has been burned, and the bodies of the ducks have their first layer of squiggles. Here also, the very first stage of the water has been burned in using the shader. You could leave the water at this stage if you wish.

3 Step Three: Illusion of Depth

You can see here that the dark patches have been added to the water. It gives the water a little more depth and realism. The second layer of squiggles has been added to the bird bodies, and the heads have their first layer of burning.

4 Step Four: Final Touches

The project comes to a close. Here, the last layer of squiggles has been added to the bodies. A touch of darkness has been added behind the bill and under the chin of each bird, and a blush has been added to color the wings and tails. The mid-tones have been added to the water.

For a touch of realism, try adding some reflections of the reeds in the water. A lazy zigzag line, trailing from the bottom of the reed, is all that is needed to give the impression of reflection. In keeping with the smooth appearance, a shading nib should be used here.

Beginner's Project

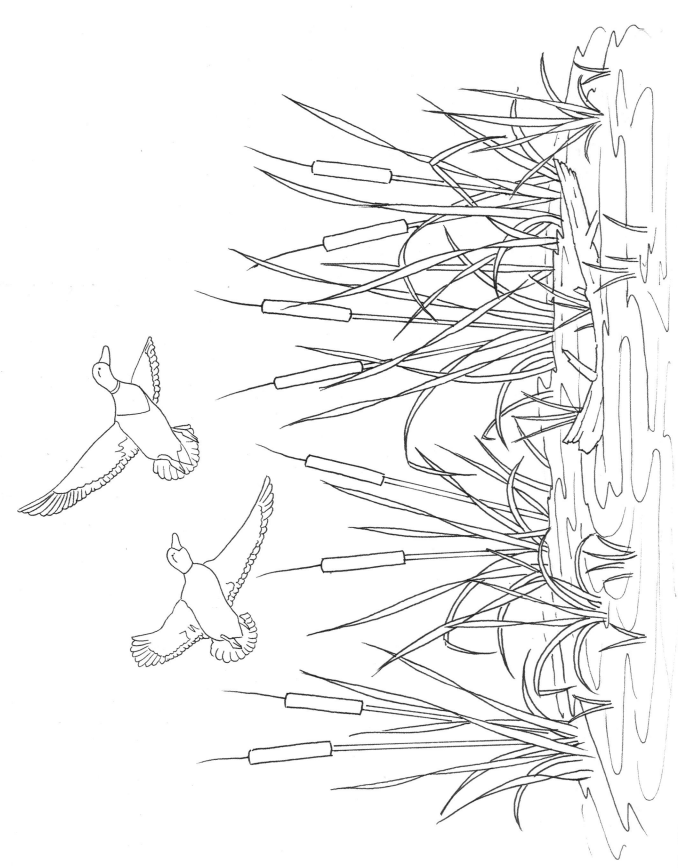

© Sue Walters

Golden Eagle: An Intermediate Project

In this project, we explore using pyrography to create a realistic picture through the use of tone and texture.

Gradual Tone

One of the most important techniques in realistic pyrography is to master the technique of gradual tone. With many subjects, it's important to develop a method that allows you to gradually build up an area of color without being able to see the individual strokes. Pyrographers haven't got a "brush" wide enough to do this in one fell swoop, so they have to create a smooth patch of color by seamlessly blending together several overlapping lines. Although this technique is one of the most difficult to master, it is essential to do so if you would like to realistically recreate objects with smooth surfaces, like human portraits, water, horses, apples, and so on.

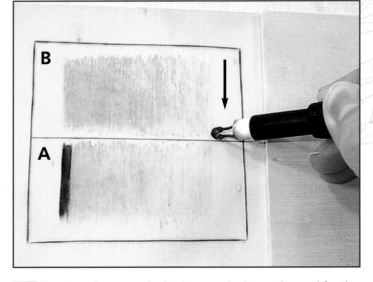

1 Here I used a spoon shader, but any shader can be used for the same technique. Use the same method of application whether the lines are curved or straight. Lines of the same color are burned next to each other and are slightly overlapping. It's important to remember to keep the nib moving when making first contact for each stroke to avoid blobbing. If the coverage looks patchy or has broken lines throughout, you can go back over those areas with the shader to even out the tone.

Remember, before attempting this technique, to have a clean nib and a finely sanded surface. These aid in the ease of nib movement and will help to develop an even coverage.

© Sue Walters

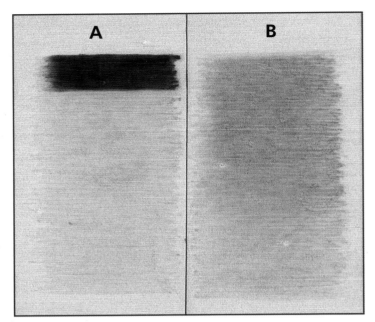

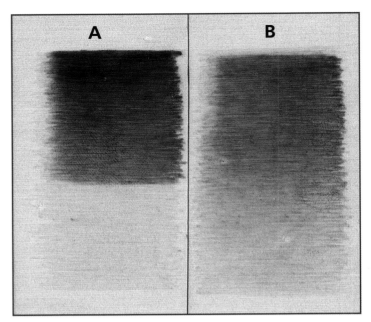

2 There are two ways to approach burning gradual tone. The first way, side A, is to burn in the darkest color, and then burn increasingly lighter layers of tone below that area. This method is effective when burning a picture that has dark areas that need to fade into the surrounding lighter tones.

The second way, side B, is to gradually build up increasingly darker layers of tone, one on top of the other. This way is especially good when burning human portraits or anything needing a subtle variety of soft tones.

3 You'll notice that I laid a very light tone as a base to side A, even though I am working the shading from dark to light. Burning reacts differently when placed on top of a scorched area as opposed to an unburnt area. Burned marks on top of a previously burnt area are lighter and react more predictably than burning on raw timber. To prevent the raw area from burning differently than the previously burned area, I covered the surface with the lightest scorched coverage to help the entire piece burn consistently.

When blending a burned area with a raw area, always try to start your stroke from the burned area and pull into the raw area, not vice versa.

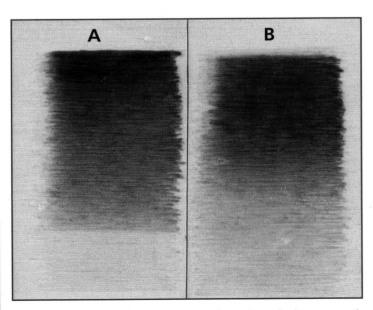

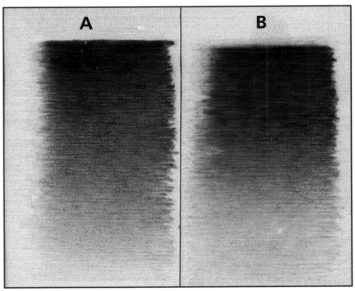

4 Nib temperature and consistency of speed are the keys to good gradual burning. It is essential that you practice developing an even stroke speed across the surface for each of the lines in a patch of tone. Developing a good rhythm helps.

Try not to lift your nib off the surface for too long between the time you end one stroke and start another. The long break lets the nib heat up too much and increases the chance of uneven darkness at the start of each line.

5 As you proceed, don't forget to use a blade to fix any mistakes, to lighten any over-burned areas, or to help blend one edge of tone with another.

Blade Use

A blade edge can be one of the most useful tools in your pyrographic kit. I personally use a snap blade, as seen in the picture below, but many other blades can be used to perform the same function, such as stencil knives, carving tools, and safety razor blades.

If held on its side, a blade can be used like a cabinet scraper and will remove an area of pyrography far better than sandpaper. Its point is used to scrape out the highlights of eyes. It's an excellent tool for lightening any over-burned areas, and it's invaluable for tidying up burn flares along a skew line or other areas. The trick to using a scraper is to work gently. Don't try to remove too much at once, or you risk gouging the wood and preventing neat removal of subsequent layers.

Here I used the blade from a snap knife to accent the white highlights on the tips of large neck feathers. I lay the blade nearly flat and scrape repeatedly, but in a gentle manner, across the area.

The Components

This intermediate project is made up of five basic components: the beak, the eye area, the head feathers, the neck feathers, and the body feathers. In the various stages, we'll discuss what nibs work best and how best to use them.

Of these five components, the feathers are divided further into four groups as explained on the following pages: head feathers, small neck feathers, large neck feathers, and body feathers. The construction of each of these feather groups can be broken down into three simple parts.

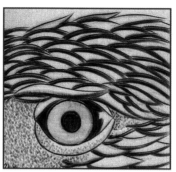

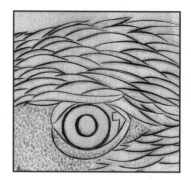

Head Feathers

1   To create a crisp, well-defined line, the head feathers are outlined using a skew. Each stroke is like a tiny arch that adjoins its neighboring arch.

2   A thick, dark line is then burned below each arch. This line needs to be thick and soft, so a shading or a writing nib can be used.

3   All but the white highlights are then colored in by sweeping a shader over the top of the previous burning.

The Eye

1   Outline the eye with a skew. Because a skew can be difficult to turn in a tight circle, you may want to use a writing nib to burn the pupil and iris areas. To burn a neat circle it is often better to work in short strokes, overlapping the end of the previously burnt line and extending it a little farther on the next stroke. Keep turning the board and work the nib toward yourself.

2   Fill in the black parts using a shading nib or a writing nib. Because the eye is smooth, a shader is used to add just a touch of soft color to the iris.

3   Lastly, use the shader to burn a ring of slightly darker color around the iris. (You might want to use a writer for this if you feel your shader is too large.) A shader is also used to add a blush of shade under the eyelid. The highlight is scratched out. You can also create the highlight by leaving this area unburned.

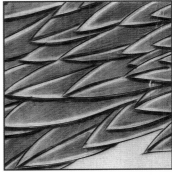

Small Neck Feathers

1 The small chin and neck feathers are also outlined with a skew. These feathers form intersecting Vs. The small loops below the beak are best burned with a writer because of their tight curves.

2 As done on the head, burn a dark line under every line and under the loops.

3 Except for the highlight, color the whole area over in a mid-tone with a shader. Once this is done, add more darkness under the chin to emphasize its being in the shade. You may have to turn up your nib heat to make an impression on the previous burning.

Body Feathers

1 The structure of the body feathers is also outlined with a skew. A dark, soft line is burned below the bottom skew line of the feather and above each quill line. This is the shade line that emphasizes each feather overlapping the one below, casting a shadow beneath.

2 To color the feather, we start the stroke at the overlapping V, coloring the full area of the feather in one tone, leaving only an untouched area along each outer edge and below the quill line. It's important to start the stroke at the V junction where the other two feathers overlap it, burning from this point along the length of the feather. This color needs to be slightly darker than that on the large neck feathers, so be sure to test your nib heat on your practice board before starting.

3 We need to add more shading to the base of each feather where other feathers are overlapping it. As with the large neck feathers, we do this by burning short, staggered dark lines from the V outward. This time, however, extend the darker areas along the length where any other feathers are overlapping it.

Large Neck Feathers

1 The large neck feathers are once again outlined with a skew. Using a shader once again, a soft dark line is then burned below the lower skew line of each feather. Again, this shade line will indicate shadow being cast by the top feather on the feather it overlaps, giving a sense of depth and realism. The top skew line is to be left alone. A shade line is also burned along the side of each quill line.

2 Once the dark shadow lines are burned, use a shader to add a blush of color to each feather using a shading nib. It's important to start the stroke at the V junction where the other two feathers overlap it. Burn outward, along the length of the feather, but let the stroke taper off before it reaches the end, leaving the end untouched. If you make a mistake and leave the length of a stroke too short, don't be tempted to try to repair it halfway along the feather. This fix will only create a patchy look. It is better to go back to the V and redo the line from there.

3 To further define the shadows of the overlapping feathers, we need to add a little more darkness to the areas where they overlap. Using a shader, add another layer of burning from the V outward, but this time taper if off halfway along the previously burned area. To prevent creating a finishing line, try not to stop each stroke at exactly the same place. It is better to vary the length slightly to help this layer blend in with the one below.

1 Step One: Outlining the Project

After transferring the pattern, the first step is to burn each line with a skew to outline the project. Because feathers have a sharp edge, the skew leaves the perfect impression to represent this. Use a writing nib on any areas you might have trouble burning with a skew, such as the orb of the eye.

The outline is complete and the beginnings of the shadow lines have been burned.

The completed outlining of the head, eye, and neck regions is shown here. Note that the fringe between the cere and the beak is made up of short, staggered skew lines.

The outlining of the entire project is complete and the beginnings of the shade lines have been burned on the head.

2 Step Two: Shade Lines

Strong shade lines can now be applied to the entire project. It is important that these lines are dark so that we have plenty of contrast between the shadows and other various tones. It is also important that the shadow is burned along the entire length of the feather, not just part of the way along its length.

A close up of the dark shade lines below each body feather. Note how the bottom row of feathers has no shading.

This photo shows the dark shade lines under each line of the head feathers. Note how each dark line goes the entire length below each arc and joins its neighbor. The same was done for the small neck feathers. A first layer of stipples has also been applied to the cere of the bird by tapping in many dots with the point of a writing nib. We will build more layers using this technique to create a feeling of texture in this region. (For further details on this technique, please refer to the Fluffy Fur section in Chapter 11 on page 98.) Lastly, the very darkest parts have been burned on the eye.

The completed shading of the entire project. Notice that the areas at the top of the head, the cheek, and the neck appear darker. This is because the dark shade lines have been placed closer together in these areas.

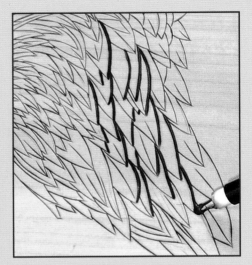

This shows the shade lines being applied to the body feathers. Note how dark they are. Here I am using a shading nib in a sideways motion to let me run its tip neatly along the edge of the line. This also allows greater motion of my hand so I can burn long lines in one motion.

This shows the shade lines being burnt on the head. I constantly turn the board so that the little arches are being burnt toward myself.

3 Step Three: Coloring In

Once the shade lines have been burned, it's time to add some color. This color should be a mid-tone of the piece. We will leave any of the lightest parts of the project untouched, burn in this mid-tone color, and then, in the next step, add more dark on top of the mid-tone to add depth and define shadow.

A blush of medium color has been burned with a shader over everything—all except those areas that we want left white. Try to sweep your shading nib in the direction of the feathers. This will help to marry the shading to the shape of the bird, even if your technique is a little patchy. Note that the second level of stippling has been applied to the cere. Only the small triangles in front of and behind the eye and on the eyelid itself have been left untouched. The iris also has a very light color across its surface, burned with a shader.

A close up of the body and large neck feathers. Note that the body feathers are darker in color than the neck feathers. For this you will either have to turn up the nib heat or move the nib more slowly across the surface.

Once again I am using a sideways sweeping motion to allow my hand greater movement. Note that I am directing my strokes along the length of the feather, not across it. It's very important to remember to try to always burn following the shape of an object. If you burn at right angles to the natural shape, your finished work will look very unnatural.

Here, the stage-two coloring of the piece has been completed. You can clearly see the different colors between each feather group.

4 Step Four: Defining Shade and Form

Once you have finished coloring, shade and form can further be emphasized by burning additional darkness. Add any last minute touches now to create a greater sense of realism.

A close up of the finished head. Note that a shader was used here to add extra blushes of darkness to the top of the head and to the throat. This is to create a sense that the head is curved and that the throat is in the shadow of the bird. At this stage several other things have been added. 1) A soft band was burned around the iris with a shader. 2) The highlight on the eyeball has been scratched in. (Eye highlights are essential to remember. It brings the bird to life.) 3) Some extra stippling has been added to the cere and just behind the eye. Extra stippling was also burned on the bottom of the lower eyelid to give it a sense of being curved and in shadow. 4) A shader was used to burn a soft blush of darkness under the top eyelid to depict the shadow falling on the eye beneath.

A detail of the completed neck and body feathers. Here you can clearly see how the added darkness in the Vs gives a far greater three-dimensional feeling. Lastly, a blade can be used at this stage to emphasise any highlights or to repair mistakes.

A close-up of the completed beak. The beak is simply outlined with a skew and then colored in. Because the beak is smooth, the shader is the ideal nib with which to burn color. A gradual build up of overlapping strokes gives the impression of curve and shadow to the beak. Note how the direction of the stroke always follows the curve of the object.

© Sue Walters

© S. A. WALTERS

FREE Pattern OFFER!

GET Creative with these Fantastic Patterns!

YES! Please send me the Free Pattern indicated below.

☐ Woodcarving ☐ Scrollsaw ☐ Pyrography ☐ Woodworking ☐ Woodturning ☐ Sewing

Name

Address   City

State/Prov.   Zip

Country

BONUS Enter your email address to recieve more free pattern and offers!

Email

Complete online for instant access to the Free Pattern
www.foxchapelpublishing.com/free-pattern

From:
City:
State/Prov.:
Country/Zip:

FOX CHAPEL
PUBLISHING

FREE PATTERN OFFER
FOX CHAPEL PUBLISHING CO INC
1970 BROAD ST
EAST PETERSBURG PA 17520-1102

Wolf: An Advanced Project

This challenging project really teaches us to expand our pyrographic knowledge.

The Components

This advanced project is made up of five basic components: the foreground, the grass, the log, the rocks, and the wolf. Of these five components, the wolf is divided into five further groups: smooth coat, shaggy coat, eyes, nose, and ears.

© Sue Walters

The Ground

The following technique can be applied to any type of ground or intricate structure—trees, bushes, or grass—that has a dark background.

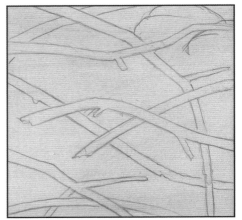

1 First, pencil in the main structure of the ground. This can include larger branches, rocks, mushrooms, pinecones, or anything else you wish to place. Be sure to make the structures long enough so that they overlap each other in places. Also, it looks more natural if most of the sticks are orientated in a generally horizontal direction with just a few being more vertical.

2 Next, sketch smaller sticks and objects under this main top structure. Make sure not to draw over the lines of the large sticks on top. Make the sticks slightly curved; this is more natural. Other objects, such as pine needles, leaves, and smaller rocks can also be added. Be sure, once again, to make the objects long enough to pass under a few of the upper objects.

3 Because these objects have straight edges, use a skew to outline the objects by burning along all of the penciled lines.

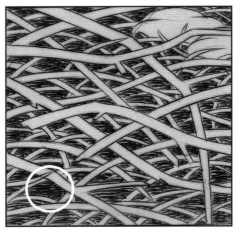

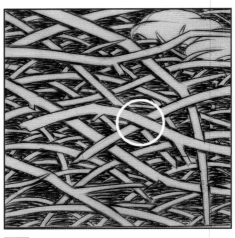

4 Use a skew to burn other small objects under the structure of branches already burnt. You can sketch these in if you wish, but this is a good time to practice some freehand burning. These objects are generally smaller and thinner than the original two top levels to make them appear farther away from the eye than the larger objects.

5 Burn any areas between the sticks darkly. You can do this by using a shader, but, since you want to create a more open structure, indicating there is yet more forest litter underneath, use a writing nib. Burn dark, curved, slightly overlapping lines as indicated. It's important to keep each stroke pointing in generally the same direction (in this case, horizontally), which is natural for the setting. This ground burning needs to be quite dark to allow for good contrast between it and lighter objects.

6 To create a sense of each stick overlapping its neighbor, use a writing nib or the toe of a shader to burn a shade line on top of the underlying stick where another stick lies across it.

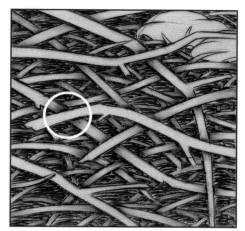

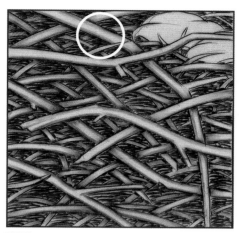

7 Use a shader to then burn a blush of darkness on the objects lying at the bottom of the stack. This should be a medium or dark color that is slightly lighter than the dark background. Cool your nib a little, and then add a slightly lighter blush to the objects second up from the bottom. Cool your nib again and add a slightly lighter blush to the objects third up from the bottom. The top sticks are left untouched. You are trying to create an illusion of light receding as it goes deeper into the pile. This illusion gives a sense of depth to the viewer. The shader can then be used to pull short, trailed-off strokes from the dark overlapping shade lines that were burned previously. This helps to blend the shadows along the sticks and also to further enhance the feeling of one object passing beneath another.

8 Use a shader to add a soft line of color to both sides of the major objects. This gives them a sense of being rounded in shape.

9 Lastly, use a skew or a writing nib to burn in some characteristics on the objects. In this case, I have burned random, semi-curved nicks to simulate birch branches. It's not overly important to make these nicks exactly perfect or to try to place them in exactly the right spot. We are only trying to create an illusion of character: knot holes, cracks, wood grain, or anything else can just as easily be burnt with just a few flicks of a nib.

The rocks have been burnt using the same method as described on page 81.

The Grass

Grass is another problem child for a lot of pyrographers. When burning grass, most of us, at one time or another, have ended up with an unappealing soup of dark slashes.

Broad-Leafed Grass: Broad-leafed grass looks a lot like strap leaves, only smaller. Please refer to Chapter Eight: Ducks and Bulrushes for a detailed description on how to burn this type of grass.

Short Grass: Burning short grass can seem the trickiest of all. What you have to remember is that grass (or anything else) gets lighter in tone the farther away it is in the picture. Keeping this in mind, we can build a field of grass by progressively making the grass lighter as it recedes. This will give us a sense of distance and will also allow each group of grass to stand out from its neighbor, thus preventing what I call "slash soup."

Because dark strokes will show over lighter strokes and not visa versa, we need to start with the lightest grass at the back and burn our way forward. Each subsequent row that is placed in front of the preceding row needs to be darker in color, so it can stand out. The row of grass at the front is the darkest of all.

1 "A" shows how each clump of grass is made. A V-shaped clump of broad strokes forms the main structure. You can use a shader or a writing nib for this. A skew is then used to burn sharp, longer, and slightly curved lines emanating from the base of the clump. "B" shows the color and structure of the three rows of grass that make up the picture in "C."

The Log

Portraying logs and tree trunks can be a complex affair if you try to depict every single detail you see. The knotholes, splits, grain pattern, and hollows are all characteristics of weathered timber. These can be burnt with an economy of strokes and a broad approach, and the result will still looking convincing.

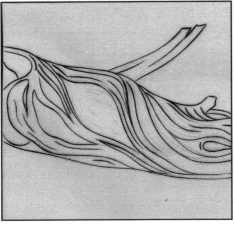

1 Using a skew, burn the sharp lines as indicated.

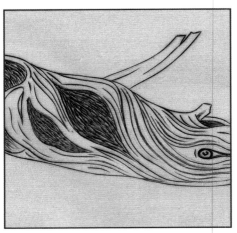

2 Create the dark cracks in the log by burning wide lines with a writing nib or the toe of a shading nib. Burn the outer and inner circles of the knot hole with a writing nib. Then, using a writing nib or the toe of a shader, darkly burn the hollows. You could use a shader to fill these areas with a solid black burn, but this would give no sense that there is something inside the log; the eye would hit the black wall and go no further. What we need to do is fill in the holes in a way that will create texture and can also be scratched back in parts to give the impression of light dimly hitting structures inside the hollowed log. Burn very dark, overlapping slashes that curve in the direction of the hollow. Later, we will scratch back a portion of this.

3 Now is the time to add some mid-tones. The surface of the log is smooth, so use a shader to burn a medium blush of color on the areas indicated. All of the lightest areas are left untouched.

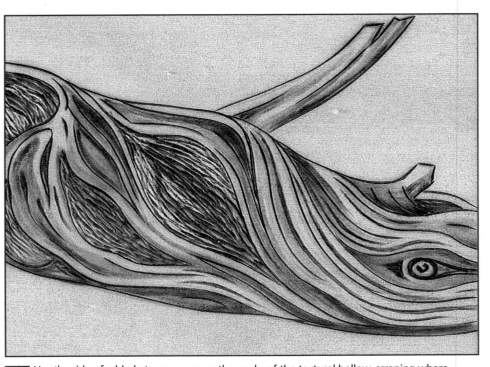

4 Use the side of a blade to scrape away the peaks of the textural hollow, scraping where indicated. Lastly, use a shader to add just a touch more darkness to the underside of the log and to any deeper dips and hollows. The edges of each dark patch should be blended into the surrounding areas to create a smooth flow between the two tones.

The Rock

Like the bodies of the ducks in Chapter Eight, rocks are a perfect example of using a nib in such a way as to impart a feeling of realistic texture to the object.

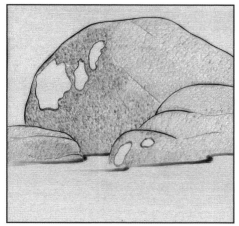

1 Because the rocks have a sharp, solid edge, use a skew to outline them. As indicated, only outline the edges of the rocks, not their ridges. Then, use a writing nib and cover the entire area of each rock in tiny, overlapping circles. The trick is to keep the tip of the writing nib constantly moving and to avoid laying the squiggles in lines. Keep the color of this first coverage quite light. You are just trying to add the lightest of colors while creating the basis of texture. It's important to try to steadily build each level of the rock, rather than trying to burn the darkest areas all at once. Here, the second layer has been added on top of the first faint covering on the left hand side. Note that the lichen patches have been softly outlined with a writing nib.

2 The entire second level of squiggles has now been burned on top of the original layer; only the lightest parts of the rocks are left untouched. The lichen has had patches squiggled onto them.

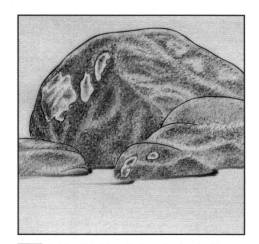

3 Add a third level of squiggles to the parts you want to be the darkest, and leave all other areas untouched. A tiny, darker patch of squiggles has also been added to the lichen to add interest.

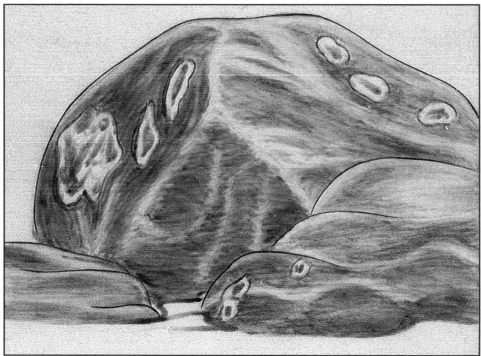

4 This is the same collection of rocks, but I have burned them using a shader. It gives them a smooth appearance, as compared to the rocks in Step 3, and clearly illustrates how using different nibs on the same subject can convey a totally different feeling.

Soft, Short Hair

There are several ways to depict hair. Here we will look at a method of burning a soft, short coat. In the next section, we will look at burning a more distinct coat using a skew alone.

A soft, short coat is effective when portraying an animal that is seen at a distance. I try to encourage people to burn what they see, not what they know is there. We know a wolf at a distance has thousands of numerous hairs covering its body, but we can't really see all the individual hairs with the naked eye. This is where the soft coat technique is so effective. We can give the impression of hair without actually showing every hair.

1 Outline the edge of the body and leg with a skew. Because few animals have a straight edge for an outline, it's important to edge the coat in the direction of the hair sticking out from the body, not in an unbroken, solid line. Try to avoid edging lines burned all in a row like little soldiers. For a more natural appearance, stagger the lines and gather some clumps into little Vs.

When the pattern is made, map the direction of the fur with a pencil. You can also burn in a few indicator marks with a skew. Careful observation of the animal's hair direction will add greatly to a realistic effect.

After outlining, burn a very light tone over the entire area using a shading nib. (See the Gradual Tone section in Chapter 9, page 66, for more details.) It is essential that you stroke the nib in the direction of the hair.

2 When we see the shade under the belly of an animal, we are not actually seeing more hairs or darker hairs. We are seeing the same kinds of hairs that are exposed to the light, except that they are lying on a darker background. The idea of this technique is to build a tonal undercoat on the body before placing the hairs on top. Here, we are building the darkness of tone by burning a second layer on top of the original. You might need to turn the nib heat up just a little to make an impression on the previously burned area. Only the lightest parts of the coat are left untouched—in this case, the area at the front curve of the leg.

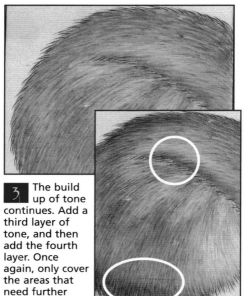

3 The build up of tone continues. Add a third layer of tone, and then add the fourth layer. Once again, only cover the areas that need further darkness; leave all other light areas untouched. It's important that you gradually build up each layer of tone and not try to burn the darkest areas all at once. For the fourth, and last, layer of tone, you should only need to burn those areas that need to be darker—the bottom, outer edge, and creases of the body.

You may have to turn the nib heat up slightly each time you add a new layer. Be sure to test this on your scrap material.

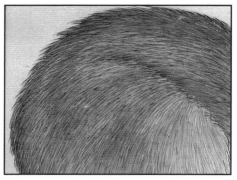

4 After the undercoat is burned, burn the texture of the hairs on top. Skew strokes laid over previously burned areas tend to be uneven and overly dark, so I use a writing nib. The temperature of the nib needs to be quite hot to burn over the undercoat.

Start filling in hair with random, overlapping, staggered lines. The length of the line depends on the length of the animal's hairs. A long-haired section requires a longer stroke. Curve the strokes slightly to achieve a more natural look and to prevent the lines from blending together. Not all strokes will burn a dark line. Some will leave whitish marks as they displace the burning underneath, helping to establish a realistic dappled, or layered, effect. Pushing hard to impart hairlike trenches on the surface also adds to the realism. There's no need to burn thousands of strokes; relatively few will produce the desired effect. Work from front to back, finishing at the edges of the coat with staggered, flicking strokes.

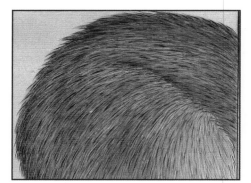

5 The beauty of using a writing nib in this method is that you are left with a series of rounded trenches impressed into the surface. Peaks are formed where the trenches join and cross each other. Use a blade to scrape the tops off these peaks to expose the raw wood underneath. Because the trenches are sunk below the scraping level, the pyrography in these hollows remains untouched, creating a very effective look of white hairs over dark.

I have also used the tip of a blade to scrape away extra white hairs. I've lightened any areas that I have overburned and marked any places where I want to strengthen the highlights.

Lastly, for that added touch of realism, I have used a skew to sparingly flick some dark hairs through the coat.

Shaggy Coat

Long coats in nature tend to clump together. If you try to unlock the tangled mess and attempt to burn every single hair, you may go insane. Most things in nature are made up of patterns and clumped hair is no exception. Once the pattern is discovered, it no longer becomes necessary to try to duplicate everything you see exactly. The general shape and any distinctive features can be traced, and the rest can be burned freehand.

1 The clumps in shaggy coats often appear like inverted teardrops. Here I have drawn this pattern in pencil and then outlined each clump with a skew. The flow lines of the hair are then burned in as indicated. (For the purposes of this exercise I have burned the background to provide a contrast between it and the subject.)

2 Using a writing nib, widen the flow lines into elongated Vs or S's. The V-shaped gaps on the bottom of the clumps point upward; the V-shaped gaps from the top point downward. The elongated S's appear in the middle of a clump. Against a dark background, these burned shapes look like splits in the coat. Here, I have only burned half of the coat, so you can see the contrast between this and the previous stage.

3 Once all of the splits have been burned, it's time to burn a shade line on either side of the teardrop clump. Where you burn this line will depend on the direction of light on your subject. If the light is coming from the right, then the shadow will fall on the left, and visa versa. Because we want this to be a blush of color without texture, a shader is used.

4 Here are the next two stages.
1) To create more hairs, burn extra Vs and elongated S's. To make the coat appear more natural and to avoid the splits running together, try to intersperse these amongst the already established splits in a zipper-like pattern. (Only half of the coat has been burned in this manner to show you the contrast between it and the previous stage.)
2) To further define the shadows, we need to add a little more darkness to the V junction at the top of a clump, where the other clumps overlap it. (See Chapter 9, page 70.)

5 You can leave the coat alone at the previous stage if you wish. To add an extra touch of realism however, use a shader to blush a mid-tone color to the tufts where indicated. This gives a three-dimensional effect, portraying some hair clumps as being higher than others and catching the light.

Eyes

There are four main components to building eyes: outlining, filling black, blushing the iris, and adding the highlight. Here I will show you in detail how an eye is formed. In your projects, however, the eyes may be a lot smaller. In this case, the four basic components are also used to make a small eye, but burned in a simplified way.

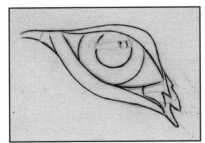

1 Outline the eye with a skew to create its sharp, solid edge. A skew can be difficult to turn in a tight circle, so you may want to use a writing nib to burn the pupil and iris. To burn a neat circle, try working in short strokes, overlapping the end of the previously burnt line and extending it a little farther on the next stroke. Turn your board to work the nib toward yourself.

I used a writing nib to burn the very top and bottom lines of the eyelids. This gives me a softer line, making it easier to blend the hair when it is added.

2 All of the very darkest parts are now burned. I like to use a shader for large eyes. A shader gives me the smoothness I'm looking for. If the eye is too small, a writing nib is a better choice.

You can highlight the eye by scratching the highlight out after all of the stages are complete. I often prefer scratching the highlight out after completion because it allows me to apply an even, burned coverage over the pupil and iris without having to work around the highlight.

3 The other dark areas are now filled in using the shader, but the color is slightly lighter than the original black sections. Note that the middle of the lower eyelid is actually slightly lighter, fading away to dark at the edges. This gives the impression of light hitting a raised, curved area.

4 Fill in the iris using a shader while avoiding the highlight. Try to curve your strokes to follow the roundness of the eye if possible. Here, you will see that I've colored the patches of the iris slightly lighter than the rest. You can either do this now or gently scrape this away later. This adds a touch of realism, because eyes catch the light at different angles and are rarely one flat color.

I have also added a touch of color to the tear duct and burned a blush of darkness across the top of the eyeball to indicate a shadow falling on it from the top eyelid.

5 The above stage completes the eye itself. It looks a little alien-like, so I have filled out the surrounding area using the soft, short hair method. (See page 82.) Here I have completed all of the levels of the tonal undercoat. Note how my strokes have followed the actual direction of the hair to be placed on top. Even without the hair texture, this creates a believable effect.

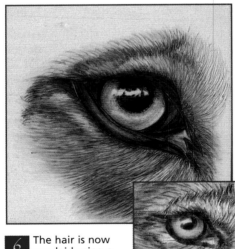

6 The hair is now overlaid using a writing nib. Be sure to start the hair strokes in the dark areas of the eyelids and pull the hair out from this area. This marries the hair and the eyelid together in a seamless blend.

The inset shows a close-up of the small eye on the project wolf. Even though it has been simplified, the eye still has the four basic components: outline, black fill, colored iris, and highlight.

Nose

Most animal noses appear smooth, so a shader is the preferred nib to use to burn them.

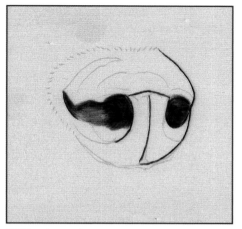

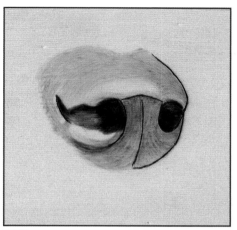

1 Using a skew or a writing nib, burn only the outer edge of the nose and the center divide. Burn the darkest parts of the nostril using a shading nib. I will often burn the very darkest parts of an object first so that I can establish the deepest tone right away. All other tones range from this color, all the way to the lightest part of the object.

2 All other parts of the nose are now progressively built up using a shader.

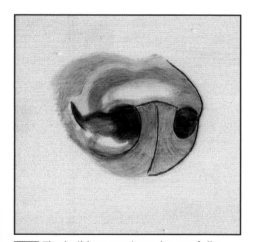

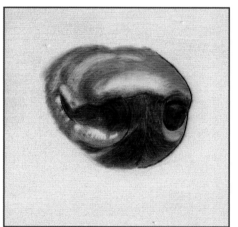

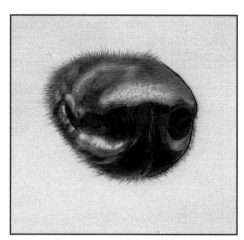

3 The build up continues by carefully burning more gentle tones on top of those already established.

4 Once again, more tone is burned over the previous layers. You may have to keep raising your nib temperature higher each time you burn a darker layer over those already established. Alternatively, you can move your nib more slowly.

5 The build up of the nose is now complete. To add that final touch of realism, a suggestion of dimples has been lightly dusted on top of the shiny highlight. I did this by tapping the bowl of a spoon shader across the surface. You could also effectively use a writing nib or the toe of another type of shader.

Ears

The make-up of ears can be a complex tapestry. Close study of your subject, noting the direction, the length, and the texture of the hair will greatly help you burn a realistic ear.

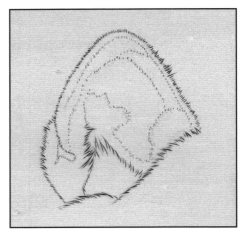

1 The edges and the main fur groups of the ear have been defined by burning with a skew. Note that the length of the strokes varies depending on the length of the hair. The strokes are staggered for a more natural appearance and clumped in a series of Vs where the hair is longer. Faint dots have been burned with a writing nib to indicate the various soft areas of the ear.

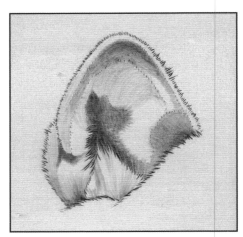

2 A shading nib has been used to build up the various colors of the undertone with the darkest area defining the recess of the ear canal. The strokes of the undertone follow the direction of the hair that will be burned on top.

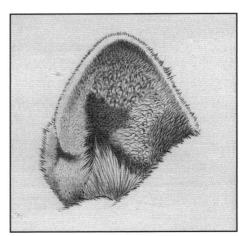

3 The initial coat of hair has now been burned on top of the undertone by using a writing nib. The type of strokes used varies depending on how long the hair is, if the hair is straight or curly, and in what direction the hair group is pointing. Because the ear canal is in the dark and the hair can't really be seen, stippling has been used to build the darkness while giving the viewer a hint of texture within.

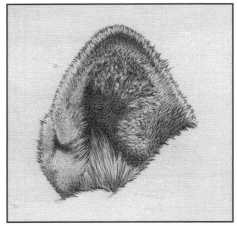

4 Adding more strokes to the areas that need to be darker has finished the ear. Note that care has been taken to blend the edges of the dark ear canal with the surrounding fur to give a soft transition line rather than a severe one.

Step One: Outlining the Project

1 Outline the various components of the project as described in the previous sections. When you outline an animal, it's only necessary to outline the parts of the animal that are of a different physical level or hair that is physically different in appearance from the adjoining hair. There is no need to outline changes of color in the coat. For example, the only parts of the wolf's face that have been outlined are the adjoining distinct hair groups that appear physically different from each other or are overlapping. Any change of color on the face within each group is not outlined. Any change of color in the coat is distinguished by tonal build up using a shading nib.

Step Two: Building the Undercoat

1 Once the outlining is complete, it's time to create the tonal undercoat. (This is described in more detail in the Gradual Tone section of Chapter 9, page 66; in the Smooth Coat section of Chapter 11, page 96; and in the Soft, Short Hair section on page 82.) It is vital that you carefully follow the direction of the hairs, as indicated by the marks on the pattern. First, blush an initial light undercoat. Next, burn a darker second undercoat, leaving the whitest and lightest parts of the coat untouched. Third, burn the darkest tone on for the final layer, leaving all other areas untouched. In this stage, you can also see that the shade lines of the shaggy coat have been burned under each clump of hair.

Advanced Project

2 A close-up of the wolf's head upon completion of the tonal undercoat.

3 A close-up of the wolf's legs upon completion of the tonal undercoat. Note how the two distinct layers of hair on the leg have been outlined as well as the toes. The changes in color on the leg have not been outlined.

4 Here, as described in the section entitled Shaggy Coat, page 83, the darker shading has been added to the Vs of the shaggy hair on the chest and on the side of the wolf. Note how much more defined the shaggy hair appears after this is done. The major splits have also started to emerge.

Step Three: Creating the Hair

Once the undercoat is complete, it's time to add hair-like texture with the writing nib. (Please see the Soft, Short Hair section on page 82 for details.)

1 This shows the wolf after all of the texturing has been applied with the writing nib to the short coat. This is enough to add a hair-like realism. You could stop at this stage if you wanted, but, later, we will scatter some dark skew cuts through the coat to accent the dark hairs that appear throughout. This picture also shows that all of the splits in the rough have been burned in using a writing nib. The coat now looks far more complex because of it.

2 Strokes have been added on top of the undercoat on the face, legs, and short coat on the wolf's side. To show a contrast, here is a close-up of the wolf's legs showing the left leg textured and the right leg untextured. The hairs have been burned in proportion to the original hairs in the reference. For example, if the hair is short, keep the strokes short.

Notice how most strokes are slightly curved. As I have said before, it's not necessary for every stroke to appear as a burned line. If the lines are too dark, they tend to obliterate the white areas. Just a medium- or light-colored impression of hair-like texture is necessary to get the desired result.

Advanced Project

3 This close-up shows the right-hand side of the face after it has been textured with a writing nib. Notice how the length of strokes is proportional to that of the animal. As an example, the muzzle strokes are extremely short compared to the strokes in areas of longer hair. For comparison, the left-hand side shows the face after dark, burned skew lines have been scattered through the coat. These skew lines were burned after texturing with a writing nib. (Please see the Soft, Short Hair section on page 82 for details.)

4 The right leg shows the completion of texturing with the writing nib. The left leg shows the additional skew marks on top of the writing nib texturing. Note that the skew marks need to be evenly scattered throughout the coat, and they should also be in proportion to the length of hairs on the animal.

6 At the end of every piece, I try to see if there is anything else that can be added or taken away to make the subject come to life. In this case, I thought the wolf was lacking some dark definition on the face and on parts of the shaggy coat. On the coat of a hairy animal, I normally add darkness at this late stage by adding more dark hair lines with a skew or a writing nib. If I use a shading nib to do this, it will iron out and mute the texture I have already built.

At this final stage, I also decide if I need to emphasize any highlights or lighten any parts of the coat. If so, I use a blade to remove what is needed. This very last stage is subtle and may seem unnecessary, but it can make all the difference in the world.

5 Here, all of the skew work on top of the coat is finished. A mid-tone blush color has been added to the tufts on the rough, longer fur at the front and side.

The completed project.

Advanced Project

© Sue Walters

© Sue Walters

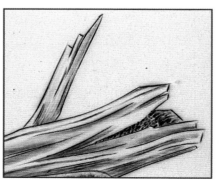

Animal Coat Techniques

When burning a realistic representation of an animal coat, it's important to select a nib with the correct profile and use it in such a way as to reproduce the texture and look of the animal. This is one reason I encourage people to push their nibs to the limit to see what they're capable of doing. (See Chapter 7, Texturing.) Experimentation gives you an excellent knowledge base for what is possible. Given experience and knowledge, there is little that can't be reproduced in pyrography.

In this chapter, we will explore vastly contrasting types of animal covers and see how the three basic nibs can be manipulated in various ways to reproduce some realistic effects.

Short-Haired Coat

There are many ways to burn the hair of an animal. Here we will learn how to burn a crisp, short coat with just a skew alone. It has a sharper, more distinct appearance compared to the soft look of the short hair technique described in the previous chapter.

Practice

Before you begin the steps, practice burning short lines in a random, overlapping pattern with your skew. To keep the lines from running together in a series of tram tracks, try to keep each line slightly askew to its neighbor. Little in nature is straight, so learn to curve each line slightly. Try to develop a rhythmic stroke, blanketing the area rather than deliberately placing each line in exactly the right place.

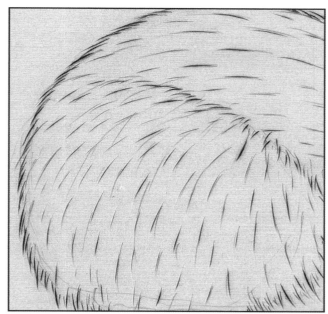

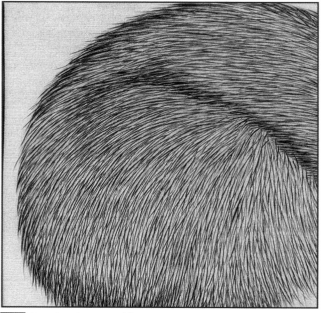

1 The edge of the body and leg are outlined with a skew. You will notice that there are very few animals that have a straight edge for an outline. It's important, when edging animals like this, that you edge the coat in the direction of the hair that is sticking out from the body, rather than with an unbroken, solid line. Don't burn the edging lines in a row like little soldiers. For a more natural appearance, it is better to stagger the lines and gather some clumps into little Vs. When the pattern is made, it's imperative that you use a pencil to map the direction of the fur onto the wood. You can also burn in a few indicator marks with a skew.

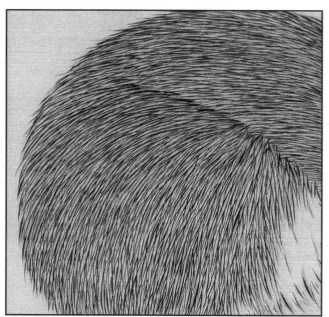

2 Here, I have burned the first layer of hair except for the front of the leg. I have left that unburned to show you the contrast between the two. Using the skew, start filling in the first layer by burning random, overlapping, staggered lines. The length of the line will depend on the length of the hairs in the animal's coat. A long-haired section of coat will require a longer stroke. Don't try to fill in the coat all at once. You can always add more hair later if you don't think it's thick enough.

3 Now it's time to add some curves and shadows to the animal by burning additional darker hairs in these areas. Try not to burn these hairs in a row; instead, burn random, staggered lines among the existing hairs. Blend the two areas together by dragging some dark strokes out into the existing coat.

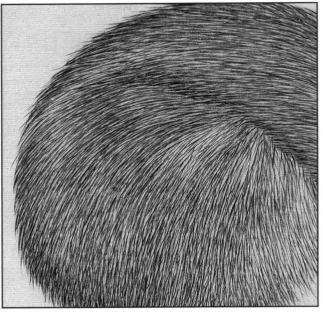

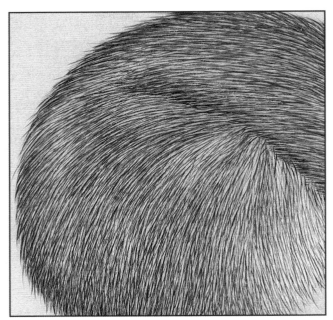

4 Once the shadows are dark enough, you can then darken any other parts of the coat by burning additional lines in these areas. We don't want the dramatic darkness of a shaded area, so these lines will be slightly darker than the original level of hair and will be spaced out so as to blend easily with the surrounding coat.

5 For that extra touch of realism you can use a blade to scrape away any areas you think need to be defined or are too dark.

Smooth Coat

I try to encourage people to burn what they see, not what they think they see or what they know is there. Just because we know a horse has hair doesn't mean we see that hair. Some animals, especially when viewed at a distance, appear to have a coat as smooth as an apple.

Practice

Please see the Gradual Tone section in Chapter 9 for additional information about this technique.

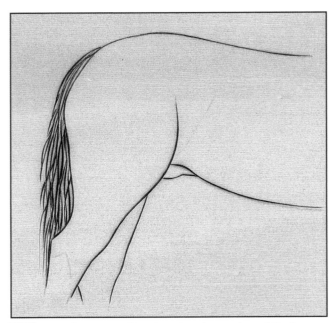

1 Use a skew to outline the crisp, sharp edge of the horse. Outlining is only used to define physical things but not for changes in color. For instance, the leg or outside rump of the horse is edged, but no change of coat color or shading is edged.

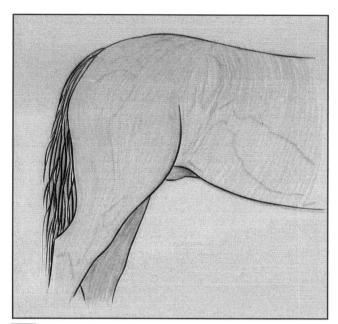

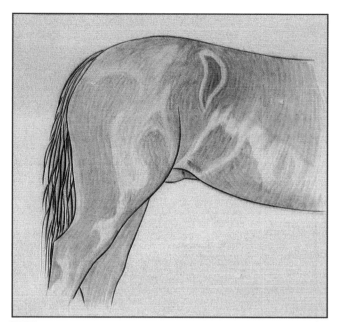

2 | Here the distinctive changes of color on the coat have been mapped lightly with pencil. The entire coat has been very lightly toned all over with a shading nib. I use a shading nib because I want to create a smooth texture. For a much more realistic look, it's important to curve the overlapping tone lines along the shape of the body. Even if your stroke work is a little patchy, this helps to marry the burning to the shape of the animal.

3 | Like water, the darker, distinctive shapes are then filled in with the shader. Always make sure that the strokes follow the lines of the first level. (Follow the shape of the animal.) If you have to, tip your shader on its toe to fill in and blend any patchy areas.

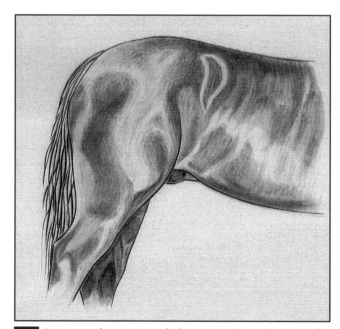

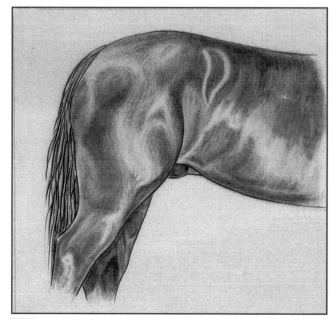

4 | Any areas that are very dark are now burned on top of the original two layers. Gently add another patch of darkness on these areas, making sure to blend any hard edges between two contrasting tones. You may have to turn the heat up a little to make an impression on top of previously burned levels.

5 | Lastly, use the shader to gently fill in any mid tones, leaving only the highlights on the coat untouched. You can use a blade to gently scrape away any mistakes or to re-establish highlights. A blade is also useful to dull any areas burned too darkly or to blend the edge between two contrasting tones.

Animal Coat Techniques

Fluffy Fur

One of the techniques I am most often asked about is how to burn fluffy fur. Fur that comes out at you can look very complex to burn, but, in fact, it is quite simple—although time consuming. We can depict this type of fur by using pointillism. Pointillism (sometimes called stippling) is the means of creating a picture by dots or small strokes. Even though it's laborious, the slow build up of this technique often ensures fewer mistakes are made. Here, we will study this technique by burning the arm of a koala. (See page 2 for a photo of the complete piece.)

Practice

Practice tapping the point of a writing nib in a random, evenly spaced manner. Try not to burn the dots too dark or in rows. Don't be afraid to tap heavily to add a physical texture to the piece as well as a visual one. Try to develop a rhythmic, tapping pattern rather than placing each dot perfectly.

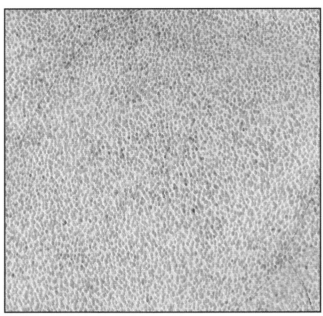

1 If we follow the principle that the length of a burned stroke should match the length of the hair on the subject, then fluffy fur really has no length at all. All you can see are thousands of dots of hair protruding from the body. Keeping all of this in mind, one way to represent this type of hair is to recreate the texture and length by overlapping thousands and thousands of dots. The perfect tool for this job is the point of a writing nib. The color of the first layer is quite light. We are really only trying to convey a touch of color while creating a physical impression on the surface. Note how evenly spaced the dots are with no one area being overly saturated. Also note that only a light pencil mark indicates the shape of the koala.

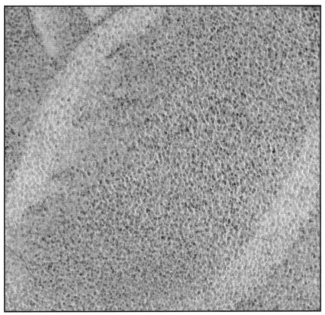

2 All but the brightest areas are then re-stippled in the same manner. You may have to turn the heat up a little more to enable you to make an impression over the first layer of burning. Resist the temptation to darken any area too quickly. It's very important that each level is gently built over the last. This helps blend each level and also greatly adds to the feeling of the depth of the coat.

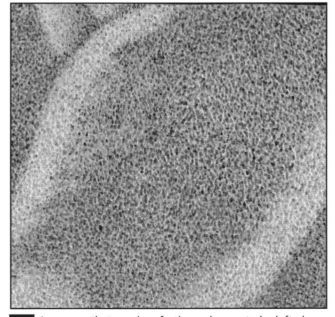

3 Any areas that need no further color are to be left alone. All areas that need to be darker are then re-stippled over that entire area. Once again, you may need to turn the heat up on each subsequent level. Notice how the gradual build up of levels is starting to add a real sense of depth to the coat.

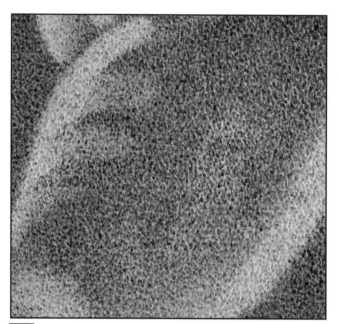

4 Once again, another layer of stippling is added only where the object needs to be darker. Notice how this additional layer of dots has defined the shape of the arm. The background behind the arm has also been darkened on each subsequent level.

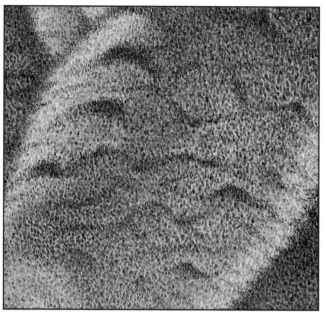

5 At long last, the final dark layer can be added. By this stage, the only dark areas to be filled in are the background and the gaps on the Koala's coat. If any levels seem to stand out from their surrounding areas, blur the edges by using a few dots to blend the two patches of tone together. A blade can then be used to highlight areas as needed.

Leathery Skin

Burning the look and texture of elephant skin illustrates just how versatile pyrography can be when you choose the right nib for the right job and use it the correct manner. Like the koala fur in the previous section, the skin of the elephant is created by building up a series of dots. Instead of using a writing nib, which creates a tight pattern, we will use the bowl of a spoon shader to dab on layers of fat splodges.

Learning the capabilities of your nibs and the patterns they can produce is the key to recreating unusual looks like this leathery skin. That is one reason I encourage all pyrographers to practice their texture squares, as seen in Chapter 7, page 54.

This technique is not limited to elephants alone. Some other things it can reproduce are reptiles, leathery human skin, and other tough-skinned mammals. Here, we will study this technique by burning a portion of an elephant eye and surrounding skin. (See page 10 for a photo of the complete piece.)

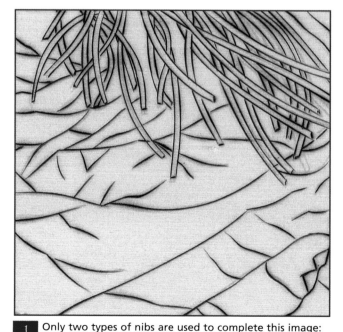

1 Only two types of nibs are used to complete this image: a skew and a spoon shader.
First, the skew is used to deeply burn the outline of all the eyelashes. Take care not to cross over lines where the eyelashes overlap or underlap one another. The creases of the skin are also burned using a skew.

2 In order to be able to stipple over the entire picture without obliterating the eyelashes, I used a miniature rotary machine and a bur to carve out a smooth trench between the burned lines of each eyelash. This drops the level of the eyelashes below that of the burning surface and it should remain untouched during the burning process.

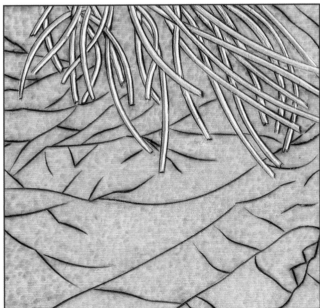

3 Tap the bowl of the shader all over the entire piece in a random, overlapping pattern. Use only a light color for this first coat. Like the koala, we are trying to establish texture, rather than heavy color.

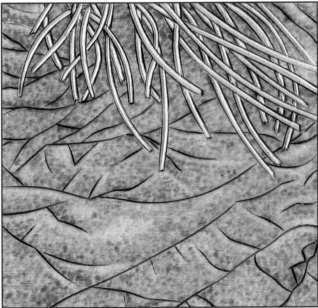

4 Turn the heat up slightly to allow you to make an impression over the initial layer of burning. Stipple a slightly darker layer over the entire piece, but leave alone any areas that are to remain brightest, such as those where the light is catching the peaks of the protruding skin.

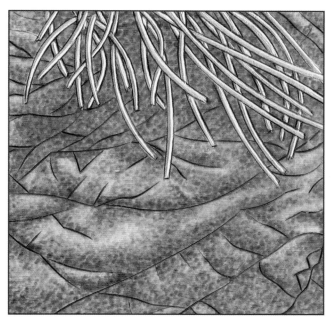

5 | Turn up the heat slightly again to stipple another layer on the areas that need further darkening; any other areas are now left alone. It's important that you don't try to build the darkest areas all at once. It is better to gradually build each level of darkness to create a sense of depth and to allow for smooth blending.

6 | Add yet a further layer of dark stipples to any areas that need it. In this case, those areas are the dips in the creases and the area under the eyelashes.

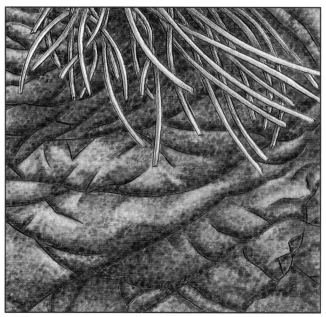

7 | Last, stipple the last dark lines right along each crease. This creates a strong shadow that emphasizes the depth of the crease. A skew is then used to darken any underlying eyelashes. (A writing nib can also be used if it can fit into the tight gap of the engraved trench.) For added realism, a dark shadow line can be burned on the lower hair where the top hair crosses over it.

Animal Coat Techniques

Color

There are three schools of thought when it comes to mixing pyrography and color. On one hand, there are purists who believe pigments should never be combined with pyrography under any circumstances; the picture should comprise burning techniques only. On the other hand, some burners extensively use color in combination with pyrography and feel it plays a vital part in their work. Then, there are people like me, who think, depending on the situation, both color and monochrome (no added color) pyrography are relevant. I think that monochrome pyrography, just like black-and-white photography, has a charm and mood all its own and can look exceptionally effective given the right subject matter. I also believe that certain subject matter can greatly benefit from the use of color. After all, a sunset isn't quite a sunset without the use of color.

There are basically three ways to combine color with pyrography: 1) Place the pigments around the pyrography on the unburned portions of the wood, 2) place the pigment on top of the pyrography, and 3) burn on top of the pigment.

As I have written in the Safety section of Chapter 1, there are some pigments that are unsafe to burn over because heating these pigments can release dangerous toxins. At the time of this book's publication, I am unwilling to advocate the use of specific pigments in this practice because I have been unable to establish exactly which could be considered safe. For this reason I won't be illustrating the use of burning on top of pigments in this chapter.

The Pigments

Oil paint, acrylic paint, watercolor paint, gouache paint, colored pencils, wax pencils, inks, and timber stains can be used to color wood in conjunction with pyrography. Even though these are the most commonly used, there is no reason to discount others pigments, such as pastels and dyes, or other techniques, such as airbrushing. You really are limited only by your imagination.

By learning how each pigment will react when applied to timber or when combined with pyrography, you can both select a pigment that best suits the effect you are trying to achieve and avoid the pitfalls of using unsuitable pigments for your projects. For instance, acrylics are effective in painting over burnt areas but, because of their transparent nature, watercolors are not. In this chapter, we will be looking at two methods of adding color to pyrography and what pigments are suitable for each technique.

Sealing

Some colors, particularly red, can bleed when varnish is brushed on rather than sprayed. When selecting a spray varnish, I strongly recommend that you test it on a sample board of your pigments to make sure the colors remain unchanged. I have found that certain brands can tend to make white paint semi-transparent. I prefer to use a solvent-based acrylic spray, but any type of varnish can be used to finish colored pyrography.

Coloring Around Pyrography

Pyrography forms a natural barrier to liquids. If you try to paint a thin wash on top of an area burned with a shader, you will find that the paint won't be easily absorbed into the surface; instead, the liquid tends to bead and sit proud on top of the scorched area. This barrier to liquid can be used to your advantage by using pyrography to line areas of raw timber (or other materials) that you want to paint. This is especially useful when considering projects that have a bold and colorful composition. Folk art patterns (tole painting), Celtic work, geometric design, and signage are some examples where this technique is particularly effective.

When the area to be painted is edged by burning, a moat is created between it and the raw wood. A steady hand isn't required to paint up to this edge because the burned area rejects the paint while the paint is easily absorbed into the unburned areas.

Opaque paints such as gouache (often called folk art paint) and acrylics are perfect for this type of coloring. They cover the surface in rich and vibrant color, and the timber is unable to show through the coat. They are also extremely easy to apply and fast drying.

Frankly, any pigment can be used for this technique. The resulting effect will depend on how the pigment reacts with the timber surface.

- Watercolor paints will leave a more subtle color, allowing some of the timber to show through.
- Inks tend to also allow the grain to show through but can be extremely vibrant in color.
- Timber stains create a more natural and earthy look.
- Oil paints can be suspended in mineral spirits and washed on much like watercolors, but if they are suspended in linseed oil, the effect can be streaky and takes time to dry.
- Artist pencils can also be used, but they tend to give a muted and soft appearance.
- Wax pencils can be made liquid after they are applied by adding mineral spirits to the pigment with a cotton bud or a brush. (The mineral spirits "melt" the wax pencil.)

House and other signage can be extremely effective when color and pyrography are combined.

The sample project in this case is a Celtic design. I transferred the image to the plywood using graphite paper and edged all but the circles with a skew. The circles were edged using a writing nib. I stippled with the point of a hot writing nib to fill in the black areas. These areas can be burned using any nib or texture you like, but I especially like the richness and satin appearance that stippling gives.

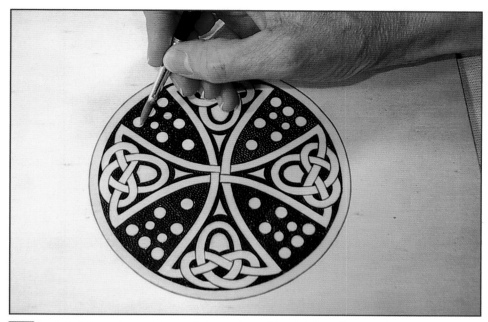

1 I painted the unburned areas of the project with a bright yellow acrylic wash. Because it's easy to paint up to the edge of the pyrography without making mistakes, quite a large brush can be used on a relatively small area.

2 In this case, I brushed a thin yellow wash (yellow acrylic paint thinned with water) over any unburned areas. Try not to load your paintbrush too heavily, or some of the paint might spill over onto the burned areas. If this happens, you can blot the excess paint away with a tissue before it dries.

3 I then applied a layer of orange wash to the outer shield and the dots, leaving the center and outer ring untouched.

4 Next, I applied a wash of orange-red farther out on the shields and the circles. Note that I have feathered the edges of each overlapping color so that they gently blend into one another. Quite a dry brush is needed to do this.

5 Lastly, I applied a wash of red to the outer edges of the shields and the circles. The bright colors look particularly effective in contrast to the rich, dark burning.

Color

Coloring over Pyrography

It is possible to add color over the top of pyrography, if the correct pigments are used. This practice is particularly effective if the timber has been heavily textured by pyrography and the paint is applied with a dry brush, allowing the pigment to catch the peaks of the texture while leaving the burned valleys untouched. (A dry brush has most of the excess paint wiped from the bristles.) This technique is especially useful when portraying heavily textured subjects like animal fur or bird feathers.

Fluid applications of paint can also be liberally applied so that the paint covers the peaks while also falling into the valleys. This leaves a picture with the impression of texture but a full covering of color.

Applying color over pyrography can also greatly enhance burning on dark wood. Pyrography stands out well on pale surfaces but poorly on dark ones. To help the design be seen, color is often used in conjunction with pyrography on darker timbers.

The best pigments I have found for this technique are acrylic and gouache. Being opaque, both cover burned areas easily and both can be dry brushed on top of peaks, as described in the illustrations following. Watercolor and ink are less suitable, owing to their transparent nature.

Pencil is also less satisfactory because the pigment tends to catch on the edges of skew work, leaving messy deposits throughout the work. However, some success can be had with wax pencil if the wax is made liquid after application by brushing mineral spirits over the pencil marks. (The mineral spirits melt the pigment.) I have not tried oil paints with this technique, but due to their semi-transparent nature, they may not cover the surface well.

Another technique used to apply pigment over burning is to seal the surface with spray varnish after the design has been burned. Once the piece is well sealed, color can then be applied to the top of the varnish. The piece is then varnished again to seal in the color.

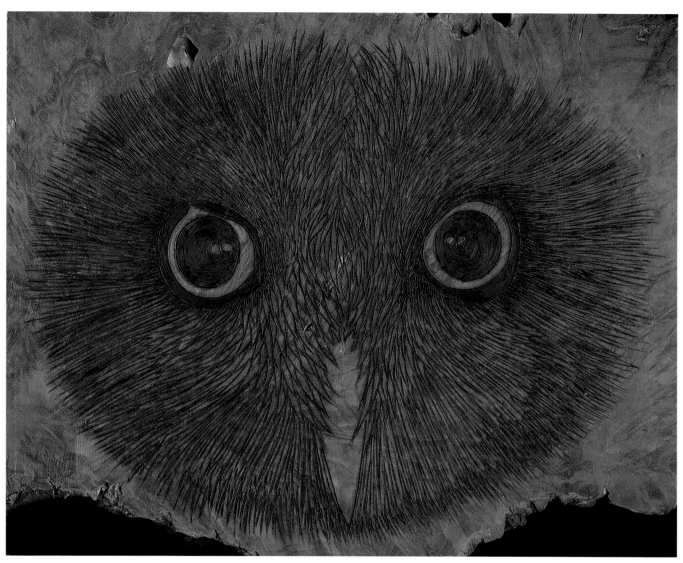

The sample project in this case in an owl face. It was burned on a piece of mallee, which is a dark, dense Australian timber. The eyes were burned black using a shading nib, making sure to leave the highlights untouched. All of the feather texture was then heavily burned, or cut in, using a heavy-duty skew. (A heavy-duty skew was necessary because of the hardness of the timber. A normal skew can be used for softer woods.) Extra heavy skew lines, placed close together, were used to emphasise the darkness around the eyes and the dark patches radiating outward on the face. At this stage, I was simply trying to burn the texture of the feathers rather than burn a realistic picture. (Have faith. At this stage, the project looks a mess, but it will improve.)

The owl face on dark timber after the pyrographic stage.

Color

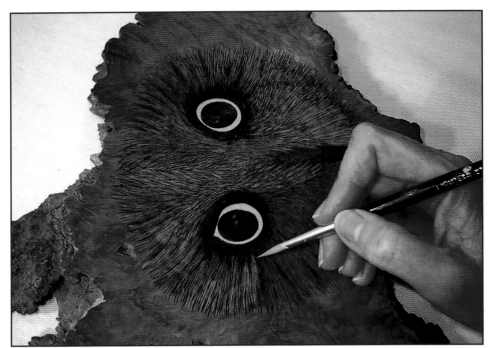

2 This is the owl face after the first application of paint. The eyes have been painted with yellow acrylic paint and the beak has been burned a smooth black with a shading nib. You will find that some paint inevitably falls into a random valley. This doesn't matter at all. The texture of the line still remains, giving the impression of feathers. And therein lies the beauty of this technique. If you are a poor painter, it doesn't matter because you have already established the structure of the face and the texture and direction of feathers with your burner. It's not necessary to know how to paint in every feather or hair, you simply now have to "dress" the skeleton you have already created. (Notice that the dark areas around the eyes and the beak have remained unpainted.)

1 I applied the first layer of paint with a fairly dry brush. In this case, I used yellow ochre acrylic paint. If the paint is lightly brushed over the surface of the pyrography, it will catch on any peaks of unburned wood and leave the burned valleys untouched. It's important to brush in the direction of the burned lines and not across them. Note: Once the texture has been burned, it's important that you brush away any soot and dirt before painting. A small wire brush is ideal for this step.

3 I then dry brushed a second layer on the outer edge of the mask and between the eyes using burnt sienna acrylic paint.

4 Next, I dry brushed white acrylic paint over the feathers where indicated. It might take several applications of white paint to cover the previous color sufficiently. In this case, three layers of white were applied. Two dabs of paint were added to the unburned highlight of the pupils, and a thin white line was painted around the edges of the eyes. White has also been dry brushed onto the beak to represent reflected light.

5 I completed the piece by adding extra white to emphasize the bright feather areas above the eyes, around the top of the beak, under the eyes, and around the fringe. A streak of white was added to the yellow of the eyes. I emphasized the black bars radiating from the face by painting streaks of black acrylic. Black paint was also sparingly flecked over the white areas at the top of the beak and on the forehead. Lastly, I streaked a few dashes of white through the colored mask. Note that some of the dark cut marks can still be seen throughout the paint. As previously written, you can totally cover the pyrography with paint if you wish, but I find that letting some of the pyrography show through greatly helps to indicate the structure and direction of the feathers. This technique is also very effective when burning and coloring animal fur.

Troubleshooting

Like anything, one of the best ways to learn how to avoid mistakes is to make them in the first place. The trick is to then work out why it happened and how to avoid the error in the future.

By examining the following common mistakes you may be able to identify some problem areas in your pyrography.

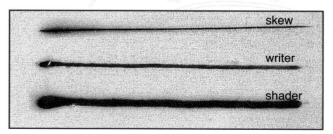

skew

writer

shader

Problem 1: Blobs or hot spots appear at the start of a line.

Solution: Think of your nib as a plane coming in to land. Just like the plane, you must be in motion when you first make contact with the surface. This movement prevents the hot nib from sitting still in one place and burning a hole before you can get your hand moving. You can then taxi (move) the nib along the surface at a speed that leaves a consistent mark. When it comes time to lift off, just like the plane, you need to remain in motion to prevent the nib from resting—even for a split second—in one place and burning yet another blob at the end of the line. You can also gently blow on the nib before contact to take some heat off it. Stop blowing on contact and proceed to burn.

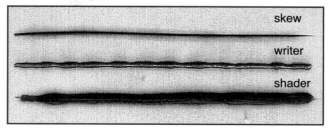

skew

writer

shader

Problem 2: Lines are untidy and blobby, and scorch marks appear along the edge.

Solution: If you have the nib heat set too high it will burn an untidy line that will show scorch marks along the edges. Burning too hot will also rapidly build up carbon and dirt on the nibs. It is difficult to repair this, but scraping with a blade can clean up the edges a little and will remove the scorch line. Use practice material to establish the correct nib heat. Set it to a temperature that burns a neat line of the darkness you want at a speed you are comfortable with. With practice, this will become quite instinctive.

Troubleshooting

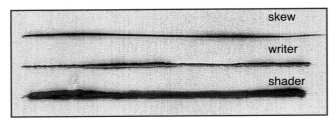

Problem 3: Lines appear uneven in thickness or color.

Solution: If you have set your nib temperature correctly but are getting burn lines that are inconsistent in thickness and darkness, more than likely the culprit is varying nib speed.

It is essential to move your nib across the surface at an even speed. Moving too fast will cause the line to lighten and thin; moving too slowly will cause the line to darken and widen. (Sometimes this can also be caused by inadvertently breathing on the nib if you have your head too close to your work.) Set your burner to a temperature that burns a neat line of the darkness you want at a speed you are comfortable with. Practice moving the nib across the surface at a consistent speed. In time, this will become much easier.

To experiment, try altering the speed as you burn a line to see how this affects the line.

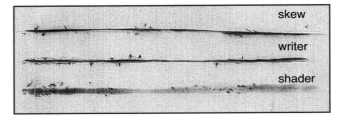

Problem 4: Lines appear dirty, and the burning is inconsistent.

Solution: Dirty nibs prevent all of the nib heat from getting to the surface, leaving an inconsistent and often dirty line. The carbon and other build up also form a rough layer on the nib, preventing it from traveling smoothly across the surface. (You can often tell when nibs are getting dirty by feeling "drag" when you try to burn.) Nibs with heavy build up of carbon can also leave debris on your project. Prevention is the only cure for this problem. Make it a practice to always keep your nibs clean of build-up.

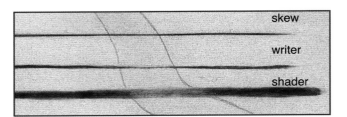

Problem 5: Work appears checkered when burning over grain lines.

Solution: The grain lines in timber often burn differently from the surrounding wood. Depending on the timber, the burn can be either lighter or darker in comparison. This can create a checkered pattern on your project, especially when viewed from some distance. Some timber, such as pine, is particularly susceptible to this. Because a skew cuts as it burns, it encounters fewer problems than other nibs. It slices through the waves of grain much like the bow of a ship does through waves of water. The writer and shader do not cut into the wood as they burn, so as they encounter each wave, they tend to jump, causing greater problems.

Adjusting your nib speed when you encounter a wavy area can help prevent this problem. If the grain is softer than the surrounding area, you will have to speed up. If the grain is harder than the surrounding area, you will have to slow down. Sometimes it's necessary to go back over pale areas and gently add additional burning to make the colors match up. A blade can be used to scrape away any grain that has been burned too darkly.

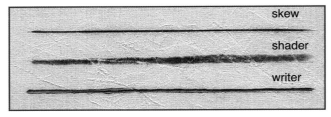

Problem 6: Work appears scratchy and there is resistance to easy nib movement.

Solution: Burning on ill-prepared timber not only prevents smooth nib movement, but it can also prevent clean burning. Once again, the skew encounters fewer problems than other nibs since it cuts beneath the rough surface. The shader tends to catch the peaks and leave the valleys unburned, creating a mottled look. (Keep in mind that surfaces can be roughened on purpose to add to the mood of a piece—think rustic or "moody" pyrography.) The only prevention of a scratchy surface is to finely sand the entire surface before burning.

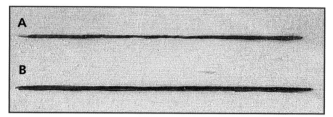

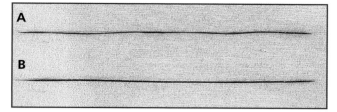

Problem 7: Difficulty burning an even, straight line with a writing nib.

Solution: It is far more difficult to burn a neat, straight line with a writing nib than it is with a skew. The writer doesn't cut into the surface, so it can skip and slide more easily than a bladed nib.

Image A: It is extremely difficult to burn a long, even line with a writing nib in one long continuous sweep. (This doesn't apply to soft materials such as leather.)

Image B: It is better to burn the line in a series of short lines joined together. Start at the beginning and burn a line only so far as you are comfortable with and in control. Lift the nib off the surface while the burner is in motion and then reapply it to the end of the previously burned line, just before the trailing tail. Continue burning the line farther and once again lift it off after a comfortable distance. Keep repeating this motion until the line is finished. It is essential that you keep the image of "landing the plane" firmly in mind when doing this technique, otherwise blobs may appear along the line. If the line is uneven in width after you have finished, you can cool the nib down a little and run it along the line to widen any thin areas. Use a blade to scrape away any bulging or ragged edges along the line.

Problem 8: Difficulty burning a straight line with a skew.

Solution: A skew is designed to cut as it burns. Once the skew is anchored in the material you are burning, it's quite easy to pull it back toward yourself and burn a straight line without wavering.

Image A: Problems occur when only the very tip of the skew is used because a smaller portion of the nib is anchored, allowing the nib to easily twist and skid.

Image B: When the majority of a straight skew blade is buried in the surface, it prevents the skew from twisting or sliding from side to side.

Using an edge to guide the nib is often unsuccessful. If a metal rule is used, much of the heat from the nib will be absorbed by the metal. However, if you raise the ruler above the nib, you can run the pen shaft along the guide, thus preventing the nib from touching the ruler.

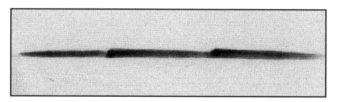

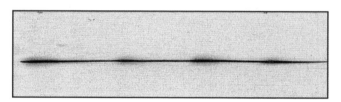

Problem 9: Blobs occur along a line or along an area burned with a shading nib.

Solution: You may experience difficulty if the nib is placed in the light tail section of the previously burned line and not slightly before it. For the next line, it is better to catch the previous line just prior to this area, where the line is dark and thick. From there, you will burn over the tail, thickening it, and continue on burning the next track.

Much the same as a writing nib, the shading nib can be a difficult tool for burning continuous long lines. It is better to burn the line in a series of short lines joined together. Start at the beginning and burn a line only as far as you are comfortable doing and as long as you remain in control. Lift the nib off the surface and then reapply it to the end of the previously burned line, just before the trailing tail. Continue burning the line farther and, once again, lift off after a comfortable distance. Keep repeating this motion until the line is finished. It's crucial that you keep the image of "landing the plane" firmly in mind when doing this technique, otherwise blobs may appear along the line.

Problem 10: Hot spots appear along a line burned with a skew or a writing nib.

Solution: Sometimes it's not possible to burn an entire continuous line with a skew. In that case you can continue the line by inserting the skew in the tail of the previous line and continuing on from there. Problems arise when the skew is placed in the groove of the previous line when the nib is too hot. This can form a series of blobs and scorches. If the temperature is turned down to manage this problem, there won't be sufficient heat to burn the next line of the same consistency as the first. To prevent this problem, it is better to blow gently on the nib while you place it in the previous skew cut. Stop your breath and continue burning the next line once heat is recovered to the nib, usually after a split second.

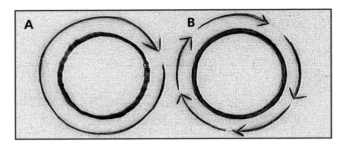

Problem 11: Trouble burning a neat circle or curve using a writing nib.

Solution:
Image A: Burning a circle or curve in one continuous stroke can result in an uneven appearance.

Image B: It is better to burn the circle in a series of short strokes. As with the problem regarding burning straight lines with a writing nib, start at the beginning and burn a line only as far as you are comfortable with and in control. Lift the nib off the surface, and then reapply it to the end of the previously burned line, just before the trailing tail. Continue burning the line farther and, once again, lift off after a comfortable distance. Keep repeating this motion until the circle is finished. Again, it's necessary that you keep the image of "landing the plane" firmly in mind when doing this technique, otherwise blobs can appear along the line. Note: You will need to continuously turn your board to allow the nib to travel in a comfortable direction.

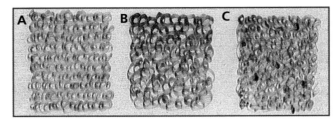

Problem 12: Inadequate coverage when filling in an area with a writing nib.

Solution:
Image A: Lines can appear among coverage of an area with a writing nib when the squiggles are applied in rows. It is better to fill the area in a random pattern rather than to continually move in one direction.

Image B: Using a large circular motion to cover an area creates a rough texture, where the circles are clearly seen. While this can be effective for some projects, it is not suitable if you want to create a smooth coverage, as seen on the duck bodies in Chapter 8 or on the rock in Chapter 10. Tighter circles will also create layers that can be more easily blended together.

Image C: It is important to keep your nib constantly moving. If you let it stop in one place you will burn dark dots among the squiggles. Lift the nib off the surface if you need to stop.

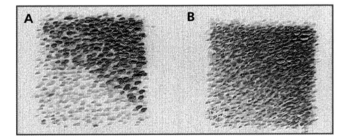

Problem 13: No smooth transition when stippling an area with a writing nib.

Solution: As discussed in the Fluffy Fur section in Chapter 11, stippling can be an effective tool to portray soft textures.

Image A: Problems can arise when patience is not exercised and an attempt is made to cover or darken the area too quickly. This makes each layer of stippling stand out proudly from the other rather than blend into a smooth cover. It also causes the edges of the transition lines to stand out starkly against each other.

Image B: It is better to build each layer of very fine dots gradually. To blur the edges where two contrasting layers meet, sparingly place some extra dots of the darker layer slightly into the lighter layer along the transition line.

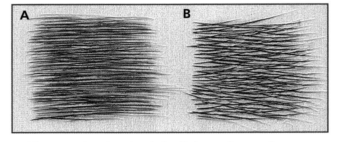

Problem 14: When burning hair, all the strokes tend to run together in parallel lines.

Solution:
Image A: When burning hair, try to avoid burning the lines straight and parallel to each other. This causes the strokes to run together in a series of railway tracks. Not only does this look unnatural, but it also makes placing additional hairs on top virtually impossible without creating unsightly black gashes.

Image B: To avoid this, try to keep each line slightly askew to its neighbor so each line crosses over the other in a lazy lattice pattern. Little in nature is straight, so learn to curve each line slightly. This also helps to prevent two lines from running into each other. It is then possible to add additional strokes on top of the lattice.

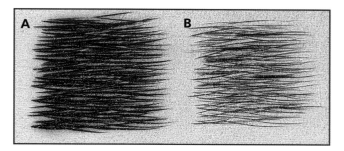

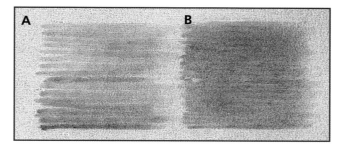

Problem 15: When burning hair, it looks like a black mass or dark lines appear.

Solution:
Image A: In Problem 2, we see that burning with a skew at high heat can widen the line and cause scorch marks to appear along the edge of the stroke. When burning hair, this can result in the area appearing far too dark. To prevent this, reduce the nib heat. (Please see the Short-Haired Coat section in Chapter 11 on page 95.)

Image B: The skew burns with the grain more easily than across it. In this case, the skew can get caught in the grain and burn a much darker line than the surrounding pyrography. Be aware of the direction of the grain and increase the speed of your strokes when burning along this line. Use the tip of a blade to gently lighten these mistakes.

Problem 16: Uneven patches or lines appear when coloring an area using a shading nib.

Solution:
Image A: Lines can appear when coloring an area with a shader. This occurs when each line isn't slightly overlapping the previously burned line.

Image B: When lines are placed next to each other and slightly overlapping, the pale area underneath can't show through. If the coverage looks patchy or has broken lines throughout, you can go back over those areas with the shader to even out the tone.

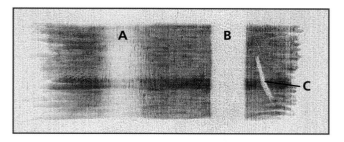

Problem 17: When fixing a mistake with sandpaper, the area appears dirty and smudged.

Solution:
Image A: When using sandpaper to erase an area, the sandpaper can leave an unsightly, smudgy trough. It is also very difficult to erase a mistake with sandpaper and leave behind a sharp edge, making precision removal virtually impossible.

Image B: By using the side of a blade to scrape the wood, you can cleanly remove unwanted pyrography on many types of timber. (Please see the Blade Use section in Chapter 9, page 69.) The flat of the blade is used to scrape away larger areas.

Image C: To remove smaller portions, tilt the blade so that only a corner or tip is in contact with the surface. The trick to using a scraper is to go gently. Don't try to remove too much wood at once or you risk gouging the wood and preventing the neat removal of subsequent layers.

Problem 18: Areas heavily burned with shader appear uneven.

Solution: Setting the nib heat too high when adding additional burning to a heavily burned area can cause pale marks, chalkiness, blobs, and uneven lines. This happens as the hot nib displaces the previously burned area, exposing the lighter tone of the wood underneath. Chalkiness appears if the area is so heavily burned that the surface of the timber begins to break up. To prevent this, reduce the nib temperature and slowly add additional burning.

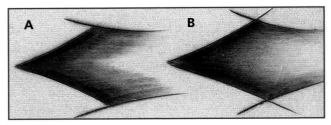

Problem 19: Layers of gradient burning don't blend together.

Solution:
Image A: Distinct lines appear when layers of gradual tone aren't blended together at the edges. The reason for this is that strokes of a tonal layer have been stopped at the same length as each other, forming a line.

Image B: To blend each layer of tone, it's important to feather the strokes of each additional layer. Vary the length of neighboring strokes to stagger the edge of the layer. It's also important to trail off each burned line by slightly increasing the nib speed at the end of the stroke and lifting it off the surface while the nib is still in motion. As with gradual tone (see Chapter 9: Gradual Tone), there is no reason why you can't go back over any patchy or unblended areas and rework them with a slightly cooler nib.

Problem 20: An inconsistent line is burned when the nib is traveling at a consistent speed.

Solution:
There are several things that can cause this problem: having your head close to the nib and breathing on it, having breeze from an open window hit the nib, having air conditioning or a fan hitting the nib, using power from a faulty power source, or using interchangeable nibs.

Patterns

This chapter contains 10 designs to help inspire further burning. Each design comprises both a line and a tonal pattern.

The line patterns can be used for transfer and let you easily see the main components of the designs. They can be used alone for simple line burnings or for color pyrography.

Tonal patterns show the light and dark areas of the pictures and can be used as guides when burning monochrome projects.

© SUE WALTERS

Patterns

Chickadee Pair

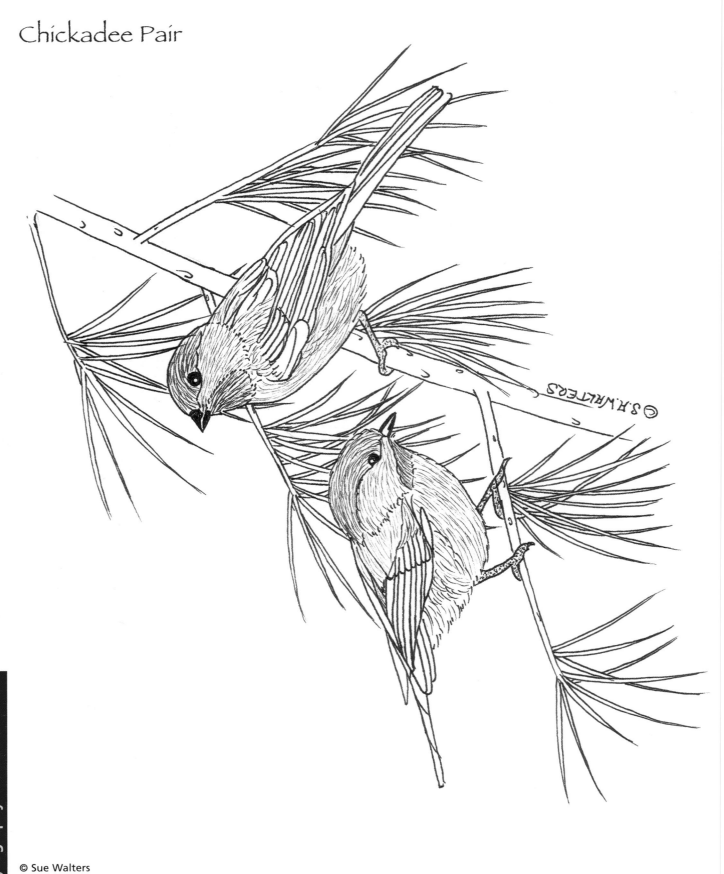

Gentle Fawn

© Sue Walters

Patterns

Night Watcher

© S.A.WALTERS

Patterns

Lunchtime

©S.A.WALTERS

©S.A.WALTERS

Patterns

Great Polar Bear

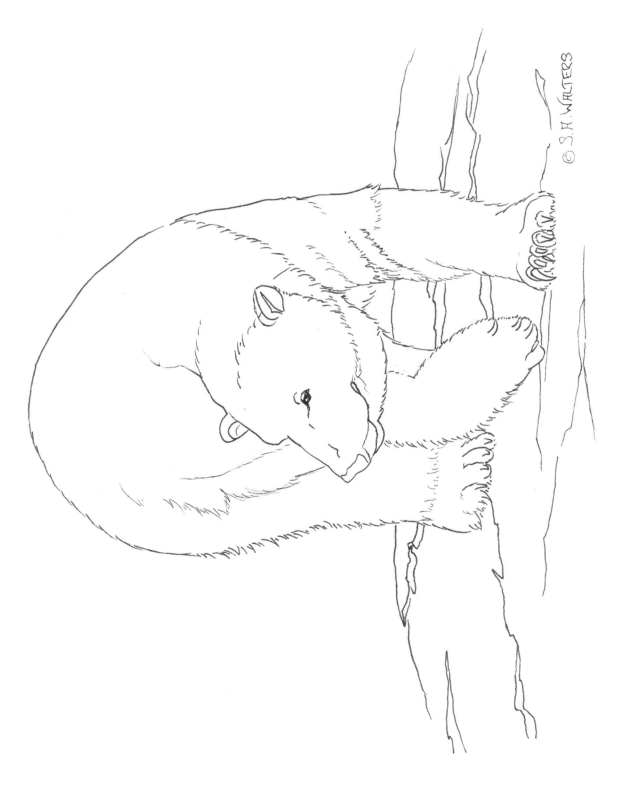

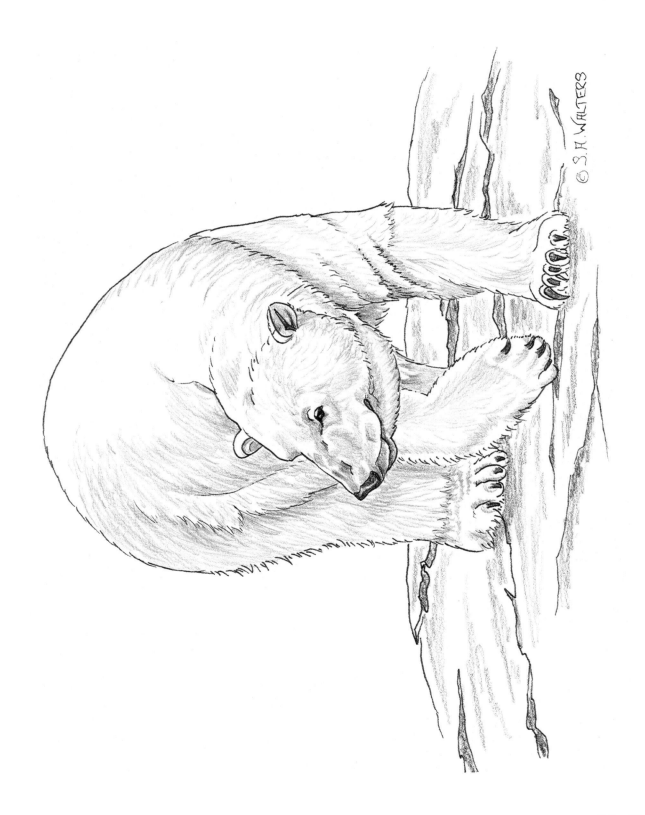

Curiosity

Patterns

Bright-Eyed & Bushy-Tailed

© Sue Walters

Silent Watch

© S.A.WALTERS

Howling Wolf

Patterns

Grazing Zebra Pair

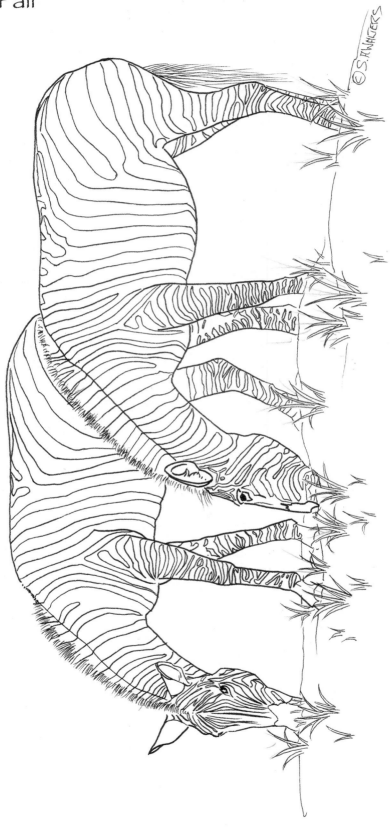

RESOURCES

Pyrographic Machines

Brenn Peter
Available at specialized
woodworking outlets.
Set temperature and variable tempera-
ture wire nib burners

Colwood Electronics
44 Main St.
Famingdale, NJ 07727
(732) 938-5556
Fax: (732) 938-9037
www.woodburning.com
Variable temperature wire nib burners

Detail Master
Leisure Time Products, Inc.
2650 Davisson St.
River Grove, IL 60171
(708) 452-5400
Fax: (708) 453-7515
www.detailmasteronline.com
Variable temperature wire nib burners

Dremel
4915 21st St.
Racine, WI 53406
800-437-3635
www.dremel.com
Set temperature, solid point burners

Hot Tool
M.M. Newman Corporation
24 Tioga Way
PO Box 615
Marblehead, MA 01945
800-777-6309 or (781) 631-7100
Fax: (781) 631-8887
www.mmnewman.com
Set temperature, solid point burners

Ironcore Transformers
20-22 Quinn St.
Preston, Victoria 3072 Australia
+61 03 9480 6044
Fax: +61 03 9416 9404
www.ironcore.com.au
Distributor: Sue Walters Pyrography
www.suewalters.com
+61 03 9754 8207

Matson
100 Links Road
St. Marys, NSW 2760
Australia
+61 612 98 333 444
www.matson.com.au
Distributor: Sue Walters Pyrography
www.suewalters.com
+61 03 9754 8207

ND1
Pyrographic Equipment Manufac-
turing
P.O. Box 331
Kilsyth, Victoria 3137
Australia
03 9724 9320
Note: Australian orders only
Variable temperature, wire nib burners

Nibsburner
Mountain Woodcarvers
PO Box 3485
Estes Park, CO 80517
(970) 586-8678
www.mountainwoodcarvers.com
Set temperature and variable tempera-
ture wire nib burners

Fur and Feathers Woodburning
121 Basswood
Springfield, IL 62707
(217) 529-4123
www.fandfwoodcarving.com
Variable temperature, wire nib burners

Optima
PJL Enterprises
PO Box 273
720 Perry Ave. N.
Browerville, MN 56438
(320) 594-2811
www.carvertools.com
Variable temperature, wire nib burners

Peter Child
The Old Hyde, Little Yeldham,
Near Halstead
Essex CO9 4QT
England
+44 01787 237291
Fax: +44 01787 238522
www.peterchild.co.uk
Variable temperature, wire nib burners

Razertip Industries Inc.
310 9th St. N.
PO Box 910
Martensville, SK S0K 2T0
(306) 931-0889
Fax: (306) 242-6119
www.razertip.com
Variable temperature, wire nib burners

Wall Lenk
PO Box 3349
Kinston, NC 28502
(252) 527-4186
Fax: (252) 527-4189
www.wlenk.com
Set temperature, solid point burners

Walnut Hollow Farm, Inc.
1409 State Rd. 23
Dodgeville, WI 53533
800-950-5101
www.walnuthollow.com
Set temperature, solid point burners

Tagua

One World Projects Inc.
43 Ellicott Ave.
Batavia, NY 14020
(585) 343-4490
www.oneworldprojects.com
Tagua slices and whole nuts

Christian J. Hummul Co.
422 Third Street
PO Box 522
Nescopeck, PA 18635
800-762-0235
www.craftwoods.com

Treeline
1221 East 1120 South
Provo, Utah 84606
800-598-2743
www.treelineusa.com

Woodcraft
1177 Rosemar Road
PO Box 1686
Parkersburg, WV 26102
800-225-1153
www.woodcraft.com

Gourds

Gourds Downunder
Bronii Williams
17A Coal Point Rd.
Coal Point, NSW 2283
Australia
02 4959 7042
www.gourdsdownunder.com
Australian gourd information

The Canadian Gourd Society
www.canadiangourdsociety1.
homestead.com
Canadian gourd information

The American Gourd Society
P.O. Box 2186
Kokomo, IN 46904
www.americangourdsociety.org
American gourd information

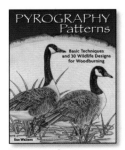

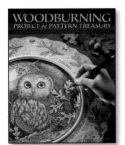
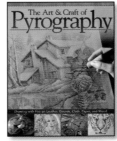

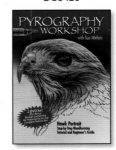